# GRUMPY OLD MEN

*Understanding the Minor Prophets*

Dr. Todd Pylant

Word of God Speak Publishing
Fort Worth, Texas
2018

Grumpy Old Men: Understanding the Minor Prophets
Copyright © 2018 by Todd Pylant. All Rights Reserved.

All rights reserved. No part of this book may be reproduced in any form or by any electronic or mechanical means including information storage and retrieval systems, without permission in writing from the author. The only exception is by a reviewer, who may quote short excerpts in a review.

Cover designed by Todd Pylant
Author photo by Rick Dalton

Dr. Todd Pylant
Visit my website at www.toddpylant.com

Printed in the United States of America

First Printing: October 2018
Word of God Speak Publishing

## ISBN-13 9781720241171

Scripture quotations are from the ESV® Bible (The Holy Bible, English Standard Version®), copyright © 2001 by Crossway, a publishing ministry of Good News Publishers. Used by permission. All rights reserved.

*Hear, you peoples, all of you;*
*pay attention, O earth,*
*and all that is in it,*
*and let the Lord GOD be a witness against you,*
*the Lord from his holy temple.*
Micah 1.2 ESV

# CONTENTS

Warning Labels .................................................................................................. 1
What is a Prophet? ............................................................................................ 5
Six Myths We Believe About the Minor Prophets ....................................... 13
    Myth #1 – Minor Means Insignificant ..................................................... 13
    Myth #2 – They Foretold the Future ....................................................... 14
    Myth #3 – They Only Spoke About Jesus ............................................... 14
    Myth #4 – They Were Only Social Justice Warriors ............................. 14
    Myth #5 – They Were Just Grumpy Old Men ........................................ 15
    Myth #6 – They Are Too Hard To Understand ..................................... 15
The Historical Background of the Minor Prophets .................................... 17
    The Prequel ................................................................................................ 18
    The Northern Kingdom of Israel ............................................................ 21
    The Southern Kingdom of Judah ............................................................ 22
    The Exile and Return ................................................................................ 22
The Message of the Minor Prophets ............................................................. 24
    Message #1 - Spiritual Adultery .............................................................. 25
    Message #2 - Hardened Hearts ............................................................... 26
    Message #3 - Injustice .............................................................................. 28
    Message #4 - Perfunctory Religion ......................................................... 30
    Message #5 - The Day of the Lord .......................................................... 31
    Message #6 - The Coming Messiah ........................................................ 33
The Message of Each Minor Prophet ............................................................ 34
    Hosea ........................................................................................................... 34
    Joel .............................................................................................................. 36
    Amos ........................................................................................................... 37
    Obadiah ...................................................................................................... 38
    Jonah .......................................................................................................... 39

- Micah .................................................................................................................. 40
- Nahum ................................................................................................................. 41
- Habakkuk ............................................................................................................ 42
- Zephaniah ........................................................................................................... 43
- Haggai ................................................................................................................. 44
- Zechariah ........................................................................................................... 44
- Malachi ............................................................................................................... 46

How To Read The Minor Prophets ............................................................................. 47
- 1. Understand Their Historical Setting ............................................................... 47
- 2. Understand Their Original Message .............................................................. 48
- 3. Understand the Difference Between the Old and New Covenant ............... 49
- 4. Listen For God to Continue to Speak ............................................................. 51
- 5. Look For the Depth of God's Wrath ............................................................... 52
- 6. Look For the Depth of God's Steadfast Love ................................................. 53
- 7. Look For the Hope of the Messiah ................................................................. 55

Micah Speaks Today ..................................................................................................... 58
- Longing for Spiritual Awakening ........................................................................ 60
- God Wants Us to Love Justice ............................................................................. 63
- Joy Comes in the Morning ................................................................................... 65
- Pillars of Society ................................................................................................... 66
- The Hope of the Messianic Kingdom ................................................................. 68
- Godly Patriotism ................................................................................................... 70
- Who Is Like Our God? .......................................................................................... 72

Final Words .................................................................................................................... 74
Resources ....................................................................................................................... 75
Other Books by Todd Pylant ........................................................................................ 76

# WARNING LABELS

When I go into my local home improvement store to get something for my latest home improvement project, which is usually not going well, I'm always looking for the older guys who work there. There are always plenty of younger workers in the store, working the registers and stocking the shelves, but they don't know much more about fixing whatever problem drove me to the store than I do. I'm hoping to find the older guy, the retired guy who spent a lifetime as a contractor or plumber or electrician and is now either filling his retirement years with part time work to pass the time or who no longer has the knees to work the jobsite anymore. Whatever the reason they might be at these big box home improvement stores, those are the guys I am trying to find. Because they know, really know how to answer my questions.

On this particular day, I was at the big box store looking for something to unclog a drain. A simple problem for sure, and there are myriads of drain cleaners on the market. Problem was that I had tried way too many of them, but the clogs wouldn't go away. Old pipes and daughters with long hair weren't a good combination. So I was looking for something new.

Fortunately, I found the man, the older man who knew what he was talking about and knew how to fix my problem. He asked me what I was looking for, and I told him of my problem. He reached down to the bottom shelf. On the bottom shelf was a bottle of drain cleaner in a clear, thick, plastic protective bag. It was the only drain cleaner product on the shelf that came in its own protective bag. He grabbed the bottle and told me, "This is what you're looking for."

As I reached to take the bottle out of his hands, he said to me, "You need to read the warning label." I nodded my head and grabbed for the bottle, but he didn't let go. For a moment, we were both holding on to this bottle in the middle of the aisle. I think we even had a moment. As we stood there staring at each other, he lowered his voice and repeated, "You really need to read the warning label."

Suddenly, I was very aware of the bottle in my hands. Every bottle on those shelves had warning labels, which I would of course ignore. But I was going to read this one. I carried the bottle out to my truck as if I was holding nuclear waste.

A man I didn't know, but whom I trusted, had given me a warning. And he had my attention.

### Why Don't We Like Warning Labels?

As a general rule, we have a strange relationship with warning labels. On the one hand, hardly anyone ever reads them. For example, a typical can of spray paint is covered in warning labels, hundreds of words describing all the things we are *not* supposed to do with a can of spray paint. Don't spray it directly into your eyes. Don't spray it directly into your mouth. Don't spray it into a fire or toss the can into the fire. And on and on.

We don't read the warning labels because we think that the average person has enough common sense to know what to do and what not to do with a can of spray paint. And if a person doesn't have enough common sense to know that, then a warning label won't do much good anyway.

So, we ignore the warning labels. We assume we understand the dangers.

Until a man whom we don't know hands us a bottle in a protective bag and repeats, "You really need to read the warning label."

Do warning labels actually work?

In 1992, Stella Liebeck purchased a cup of coffee through a drive thru window at the McDonalds in Albuquerque. Her grandson was driving the car, and he pulled over in the parking lot so she could put sugar and cream in her coffee. As she put the cup between her knees and removed the lid, the coffee spilled into her lap, scalding her thighs. She suffered third degree burns and spent eight days in the hospital while she underwent skin grafting. She was permanently disfigured from the burns and was partially disabled for two years.

She sued McDonalds claiming that the coffee was "unreasonably dangerous." She originally won the lawsuit and was awarded $2.7 million but later settled for an undisclosed amount.

However, not much has changed at McDonalds. They still serve coffee at the same temperature, which is industry standard and similar to the temperature that Starbucks and other coffee shops serve their coffee. And besides, the cups already had warning labels on them though the lawsuit required McDonalds to increase the font size of the warning label.

In effect, a McDonalds' employee handed Stella a cup of hot coffee and said, "Be careful, it's hot." Perhaps if she had not let her take the cup from her hands and repeated the warning, Stella might have listened. Or, perhaps, Stella still would have put the cup of coffee between her legs and removed the lid.

What do you do with warning labels? Do you read them? Or do you think that you have enough common sense to know not to aim the can of spray paint at your eye or to not pour hot coffee in your lap?

I think there is something inherently insulting about warning labels. They hit a couple of my trigger buttons. First, they insult my intelligence. Warning labels are the manufacturer's way of saying that he thinks I am too stupid to know how to use the product. Do you really think I am stupid enough to drink the drain cleaner?

But warning labels also hit my "Who are you to tell me what to do?" button. We all have one of those buttons factory installed on our sin nature. And warning labels, or warnings of any kind, force us to wrestle with whether or not we should trust the one giving the warning.

I trusted the guy at the home improvement store. I read every word of that warning label. I didn't feel insulted, and I didn't feel violated. I felt adequately warned about something that I didn't fully understand.

**Warning Labels in the Bible**

It shouldn't surprise us that the Bible is full of warning labels. I could give you hundreds of examples, but consider these sharp words from the book of Hebrews.

> *For if we go on sinning deliberately after receiving the knowledge of the truth, there no longer remains a sacrifice for sins, but a fearful expectation of judgment, and a fury of fire that will consume the adversaries. Anyone who has set aside the law of Moses dies without mercy on the evidence of two or three witnesses. How much worse punishment, do you think, will be deserved by the one who has trampled underfoot the Son of God, and has profaned the blood of the covenant by which he was sanctified, and has outraged the Spirit of grace? For we know him who said, "Vengeance is mine; I will repay." And again, "The Lord will judge his people." It is a fearful thing to fall into the hands of the living God. (Hebrews 10:26-31 ESV)*

That is quite a warning. The Lord will judge His people who deliberately go on sinning after receiving the knowledge of truth. And that judgment is to be feared. One would think that a warning like that would be heeded by the people of God.

But how do we usually receive warnings from the Bible?

We usually think of a friend who really needs to hear that, or we assume that we have nothing to fear because we are not guilty of said crime. And if someone tries to apply that warning to our lives, we push back with a loud "Who are you to judge me" response. We throw words of warning to other people, but we rarely meditate on them to see if we are the ones being warned.

Which is probably why we tend to ignore the single block of Scripture that is most associated with words of warning: the Old Testament prophets.

In fact, unless your Bible is very old, the pages of the Bible that are still stuck together from the printer are those Minor Prophet books that no one ever reads. We treat the twelve Minor Prophets like the warning label on a can of spray paint. The words are for someone else. I already know that. I'm smart enough to know that. I don't need to read that warning label.

I hope to demonstrate in the pages ahead that the Minor Prophets are filled with much more than words of warning. In fact, the Minor Prophets describe the steadfast love of the Lord more clearly than any other portion of the Bible. And, the Minor Prophets describe heaven in such vivid detail that it will make you long to hear the trumpet sound. But because most of us treat the Minor Prophets as little more than a warning label to be ignored, we miss all of the beauty and greatness of this portion of Scripture.

I invite you to take a journey with me, a journey back in time to the days of the Minor Prophets. I want you to come to know these twelve friends of mine, to sit down with them and genuinely listen to what they have to say instead of muting them from your social media feed.

God loves you enough to send you the Minor Prophets. Do you love the Lord enough to listen to the words He gave them to say?

# WHAT IS A PROPHET?

On May 21, 2011, the world came to an end. Kind of. Well, not really at all. Despite thirteen predictions of the world coming to an end by self-identified prophet Harold Camping, the world is still here. But right up until his last prophetic prediction, donors were supporting him to the tune of millions of dollars. Was Camping a prophet, a false prophet, or none of the above?

What exactly is a prophet?

Well, that depends on who is using the term.

There is no governing agency that determines who can use the term "prophet." Regulations govern who can identify themselves as a "dentist" or "counselor" or "accountant," but anyone can claim to be a prophet, and anyone can be described as a prophet. The dictionary officially defines a prophet as "one who utters divine revelation, one who foretells future events, one who is gifted with moral insight, or one who is a leading spokesman for a cause" (see www.m-w.com). As you can see, this definition includes a broad range of people, everyone from Nostradamus to Muhammad to Isaiah to Camping.

And in today's world, this term is quickly embraced as a self-promotion or as an accolade to honor someone with great insight. We might call someone "prophetic" just because they have deep insight into future trends of business or economics or social media. We might call someone "prophetic" because they are the leading voice for social change. We might even call someone "prophetic" just because they touched our soul on a TED talk.

But a biblical prophet is entirely different.

**Biblical Prophets**

A biblical prophet was a man or woman called by God to communicate the word of the Lord. One did not choose to be a prophet. In fact, many God called prophets didn't really want the job. Jeremiah and Jonah come to mind. And many false prophets promoted themselves as prophets even though they were not called by God.

The genuine prophet could truly say, "Thus sayeth the Lord" while the false prophet was lying though his teeth.

There are about 55 named prophets in the Old Testament, although there are hundreds of other unnamed prophets. In the earlier parts of the Old Testament story, the prophets were called "seers," but that term was gradually replaced with "prophet" or "man of God" (see 1 Samuel 9.9).

Some of the prophets were "writing prophets," like Jeremiah and Ezekiel, but the vast majority of Old Testament prophets were not, or at least their writings were not, canonized in Scripture. For instance, two of the most powerful Old Testament prophets were Elijah and Elisha, but there is no mention in the biblical account that they ever wrote down any of their prophecies. On the other hand, the Lord did command some of the prophets, like Jeremiah, to write down the words of the Lord.

There is some degree of mystery as to how the spoken prophetic word became the written prophetic word. Perhaps like the gospels about Jesus, someone other than the prophet himself was responsible for collecting and publishing the spoken prophetic words. After all, some of the superscriptions of the prophetic books speak about the prophet in third person. But just as the Holy Spirit inspired the gospel writers to faithfully and accurately record the words of Jesus, so the ones who published the prophetic words of the prophets were equally inspired.

> *To whom I send you, you shall go, and whatever I command you, you shall speak (Jeremiah 1.7 ESV)*

Undoubtedly, a prophet was called by God. Jeremiah, Isaiah, and Ezekiel each had incredible moments where God called them to be a prophet, but most of the biblical prophets do not describe how they were called by God to be a prophet. Many prophets, like Elijah, simply appear suddenly on the pages of the biblical narrative without any introduction or backstory.

The prophets primarily communicated the word of the Lord through the spoken word, but they also used dramatic gestures, silent actions, dramatic acts, or even drastic practices. Poor Ezekiel was called to lay on his side for 390 days, and Jeremiah was called to bury a pair of underwear. Their lives were as much a part of their prophetic ministry as their words.

A prophet was also an intercessor, praying to God on behalf of the people. And it was clear that the people expected a prophet to pray for them. But the prophet was also a sentinel, keeping watch over the spiritual condition of a nation. And as such, the prophet was a mediator between God and His people, speaking to God on behalf of the people and speaking to the people on behalf of God.

But the most important thing to remember about the biblical prophets is that they were not primarily foretellers of the future. Yes, they did speak of future events, but that was not their primary calling. They primarily spoke the word of the Lord as it addressed the immediate situation of those to whom they were sent.

Consider this: less than 2% of Old Testament prophecy spoke about the coming of the Messiah (Jesus), less than 5% described the new covenant age, and less than 1% focused on events that are still yet to come. That means that about 92% of all Old Testament prophecy were the words of the Lord directed at the immediate or imminent situation during the lifetime of the prophet or shortly thereafter.

Which is one reason why it is so important to understand the historical situation of the worlds of the prophets. Simply put, if we don't know the history of the Old Testament, we can never really understand the message of the prophets. And if we don't know what the word of the Lord meant to the people who first heard it, then we will never be able to apply it to our own lives either.

Which brings up the question of how the message of the Old Testament prophets relates to our daily lives. Or, to put it bluntly, why should we care about what God said through the Old Testament prophets? If we try to answer that question by parsing their words to predict the end time events, then we are missing the primary message of the prophets. It can be difficult to rightly handle the words of the prophets, but it can be done. In fact, the word of the Lord still speaks powerfully through these men and women of God.

In summary, in order to answer the question "What is a prophet," we must consider the primary calling of a prophet, the reality of false prophets, and the historical situation in which the prophets lived.

### False Prophets

Everyone knows that passwords can be hacked and identities stolen, so the good guys are always on the hunt for the next form of security and identification. Fingerprints and retinal scans have been used for years. The latest iPhones are using facial recognition software to unlock the phone. But the next wave of biometrics might get a little weird.

According to Popular Science, the next wave of biometric identification will involve the distinctively unique human ear, our individualized heartbeat, patterns of eye movement, the human nose, veins, or even body odors. The reason that biometrics keeps getting more complicated is that the hackers keep getting smarter.

The reality is that people have been pretending to be what they are not for as long as humans have walked the earth.

And when it comes to prophecy, it is no different. As the apostle Peter wrote,

> *But false prophets also arose among the people, just as there will be false teachers among you, who will secretly bring in destructive heresies, even denying the Master who bought them, bringing upon themselves swift destruction. (2 Peter 2.1 ESV)*

If the essential characteristic of a prophet is a man or woman called by God to speak the word of the Lord, then the essential characteristic of a false prophet is a man or woman who was **not** called by God but who claims to be speaking the word of the Lord. Consider the word of the Lord spoken to the genuine prophet Ezekiel:

> *"Son of man, prophesy against the prophets of Israel, who are prophesying, and say to those who prophesy from their own hearts: 'Hear the word of the LORD!' Thus says the Lord GOD, Woe to the foolish prophets who follow their own spirit, and have seen nothing! Your prophets have been like jackals among ruins, O Israel. You have not gone up into the breaches, or built up a wall for the house of Israel, that it might stand in battle in the day of the LORD. They have seen false visions and lying divinations. They say, 'Declares the LORD,' when the LORD has not sent them, and yet they expect him to fulfill their word. Have you not seen a false vision and uttered a lying divination, whenever you have said, 'Declares the LORD,' although I have not spoken?" (Ezekiel 13.2-7 ESV)*

We see the difference between a true and false prophet:

> *A false prophet claims to have been sent by the Lord, but a true prophet has actually been sent by the Lord.*
>
> *A false prophet claims to speak the words of the Lord, but a true prophet actually hears the words of the Lord and faithfully and accurately speaks those words to whom he is sent.*

> *A false prophet speaks from his own heart, but a true prophet speaks the words of the Lord even if they are not pleasing to the heart of the prophet.*
>
> *A false prophet is actually doing a disservice to the people, but a true prophet benefits the people by leading them into covenant faithfulness so the Lord might bless and protect them.*

How were the people expected to recognize a true prophet from a false prophet? This question is not just a historical one because we wrestle with false prophets even in the church today. In the new covenant age, we have the clarity of Scripture to help us identify false prophets. Those who claim to speak for God and yet contradict what God has already said through Scripture are obviously false prophets.

But how were they supposed to recognize false prophets in the years before Christ was born? There are a couple of tests given to us through the Scriptures.

> *False prophets will be recognized by their fruits (Matthew 7.16)*
>
> *False prophets prophesy things that don't come true (Deuteronomy 18.22)*
>
> *False prophets will say what the masses want to hear (2 Timothy 4.3)*
>
> *False prophets speak for dishonest gain (Titus 1.11)*
>
> *False prophets practice sin and live unrighteous lives (2 Peter 2.14)*
>
> *False prophets speak from the viewpoint of the world (1 John 4.5)*

We are commanded to test every spirit and to guard ourselves against the false prophets. But the other side of that coin is that we **are** to listen to the genuine prophets, even if what they have to say is difficult to hear.

## The Minor Prophets

What's in a name?

According to Inc.com, it can make or break a product. For instance, Clairol launched a curling iron called "Mist Stick" in Germany, even though "mist" is German slang for manure. Coors translated its slogan, "Turn It Loose," into Spanish, where it is a colloquial term for having diarrhea. Mercedes-Benz entered the Chinese market under the brand name "Bensi," which means "rush to die." Electrolux at one time marketed its vacuum cleaners in the U.S. with the tag line: "Nothing sucks like an Electrolux." The American Dairy Association replicated its "Got Milk?" campaign in Spanish-speaking countries where it was translated into "Are You Lactating?"

The label we attach to a product can make a big difference in how it is received.

And Augustine didn't do the twelve prophets any favors.

Augustine, the Bishop of Hippo in North Africa who died in 430 AD, was most likely the first to identify the Minor Prophets with that name, which was an unfortunate choice of words. Neither their message nor ministry was minor in any way. In fact, there is one interesting fact that makes these twelve prophets significant: hundreds of years before Christ was born, the work of these twelve prophets was treated as one unit.

As early as 200 BC, these twelve works circulated as a single literary work. It was written on one scroll and recognized as a single book. The Jewish historian Josephus even numbered the books of the Old Testament in such a way that demonstrates that he thought of the twelve prophets as a single work. Many scholars even refer to them as "The Book of the Twelve" instead of as the Minor Prophets.

The order in which they appear has garnered much attention among scholars. Only six of these twelve prophetic books contain enough historical data within the book's introduction to accurately place it within history. But chronology is not the only factor in the ordering of The Book of the Twelve. The other books are either grouped in similar periods of history or are linked together with common words or images. For instance, the book of Hosea ends with a reference to grain and wine, and the book of Joel opens with the locust devouring the grain and wine. Likewise, Joel ends with the Lord roaring like a lion, and Amos begins with a roaring lion.

Why does any of this matter?

We ignore these "minor" prophetic books because their message is hard to understand or because they are not easily applied to our daily lives. Unfortunately, we think of them as "minor." But the fact that they were collected as one unit and circulated as one unit and valued as one unit should call our attention to this major section of Scripture.

Their message was important enough to be preserved as one unit. May we give them the attention they deserve.

### Nobody Likes Reading the Minor Prophets

Well, that's not *exactly* true...but almost.

Crossway recently released an infographic article about our Bible reading habits. They surveyed 6000 people to learn how often we read the Bible and what portions of Scripture we tend to gravitate towards the most. And the results are not all that surprising.

One infographic answered the questions, "Which section of the Bible do you read most often? Which do you find hardest to understand?" According to their research, most Bible readers read from the New Testament over 50% of the time. And in the last month, the part of the Old Testament that they had most often read from was Psalms and Proverbs, with the book of Genesis being a close third. At the bottom of the "most read list" were those pesky little Minor Prophets, specifically Obadiah and Nahum.

But the article also makes it very clear as to why we spend so little time reading the prophets in general, but the Minor Prophets specifically: **they are universally recognized as the most difficult books of the Bible to understand.** About 45% of Bible readers identified the Old Testament prophets as the most difficult to understand of all the Scriptures.

This reality is the driving force behind this book. I want the members of my church to **not** be part of the 45% club. And I want to liberate the Minor Prophets from the bottom of the Bible reading pool. I want to help the church understand the Minor Prophets and to make them profitable in their daily walk with Christ. After all, the Minor Prophets are part of the "all Scripture," right?

> *All Scripture is breathed out by God and profitable for teaching, for reproof, for correction, and for training in righteousness, that the man of God may be complete, equipped for every good work. (2 Timothy 3.16-17 ESV)*

I believe that the Minor Prophets, even Nahum and Obadiah can be profitable to new covenant Christians today. I believe God still teaches us truth through the Minor Prophets, truth that can radically change our lives. I believe the Spirit still convicts us of sin through the Minor Prophets. I believe that by reading the Minor Prophets we are trained in the way of righteousness, the way of living and thinking and relating that is radically different from the world in which we live. And I believe that God still uses the Minor Prophets to equip us for the good work He has created us to do.

And I believe the opposite is also true.

If we neglect the Minor Prophets, there are life changing truths that we will never know. If we neglect the Minor Prophets, there are sins in our lives from which we will never be free. If we don't read the Minor Prophets, our righteousness will never reach full maturity. And if we leave these biblical books in the basement of our Bible reading plans, we will be ill equipped to do the good work God has created us to do.

Perhaps it is time to admit to some of the assumptions that keep most of us from reading the Minor Prophets.

# SIX MYTHS WE BELIEVE ABOUT THE MINOR PROPHETS

If the Minor Prophets are so valuable and so beneficial, then why do so few Christians actually read them? Perhaps it is because we have hidden assumptions about the Minor Prophets that keep us from even approaching them. And these lies we believe about the Minor Prophets make us disinterested in even trying.

So let me offer a few myths that prevent Bible readers from understanding the Minor Prophets.

## MYTH #1 – MINOR MEANS INSIGNIFICANT

Many assume that the message of the Minor Prophets is less significant than the message of the larger prophetic works like Isaiah, Jeremiah, or Ezekiel. Of course, we would never say that out loud because we know that "all Scripture is inspired by God," but the way we treat the Minor Prophets belies a different conviction. We don't read them because we think we don't need them.

I've already discussed the tragic moniker of "Minor Prophets," but we will also see that if we dismiss them as nothing more than some old guys warning God's people about the judgment to come, then we will continue to ignore them because we think they have nothing new to add. But as I hope to demonstrate through the pages of this book, the Minor Prophets reveal the love and holiness of God in ways that no other portion of Scripture does.

Neither their message nor their value to our lives is anything close to minor.

## MYTH #2 – THEY FORETOLD THE FUTURE

Many Bible readers are surprised to learn that the primary message of the Minor Prophets does not deal with events future to their own time. As I have already said, more than 92% of the message of the Old Testament prophets dealt with events during the immediate time period of the life of the prophets themselves. They were not primarily foretellers of future events. They were primarily messengers of the word of the Lord. Through the prophets, God was speaking in history and about history.

When we stop expecting the Minor Prophets to be mere forecasters of the future, we can focus on what God was saying in history and about history. And then we can hear God speak to our own times and to our own lives.

## MYTH #3 – THEY ONLY SPOKE ABOUT JESUS

It is true that some of the most striking passages in the entire Bible that speak to the first and second coming of Jesus are in the Minor Prophets, but that is far from their primary message. Remember, less than 2% of all Old Testament prophecy was about the coming of the Messiah, and only 1% was about the second coming of the Messiah and events that are still yet to come. The main message of the Minor Prophets was to call the people of God back to the worship of the One True God and to live in obedience to His commands. And that message still resonates today.

If we assume that the Minor Prophets only served to foreshadow the coming of Jesus, and Jesus has already come, then they are of no more value than yesterday's newspaper. But while they did speak of Jesus, their primary message was the word of the Lord to real people who lived in a real world. People who looked a lot like us. People who lived in a world a lot like ours.

## MYTH #4 – THEY WERE ONLY SOCIAL JUSTICE WARRIORS

The Minor Prophets certainly called the people of God to social justice. After all, "Let justice roll down like waters and righteousness like an ever flowing stream" was spoken by Amos long before Martin Luther King, Jr. repeated it. But for the Minor Prophets, social justice was a result of the people of God living in a right relationship with the One True God and being obedient to His commands. Social justice was not an end to itself but the by-product of righteousness. The lack of social justice pointed to the primary problem which was the rebellion of the people of God.

But as we will see, social justice was and is very important to the Lord. To identify ourselves as the people of God and to not share God's heart for justice is to rebel against the very heart of God who redeemed us. Social justice is an overflow of a right relationship with God, and the lack of social justice says something about our relationship with God.

## MYTH #5 – THEY WERE JUST GRUMPY OLD MEN

I've chosen to title this book *Grumpy Old Men* not because they actually were grumpy, or even old for that matter, but because we think of them that way. Indeed, the Minor Prophets did speak words of warning and judgment, but they also spoke words of hope and restoration. In other words, they said much more than just "Get off my lawn." Our faith is weaker because we neglect these words of hope found in the Minor Prophets.

## MYTH #6 – THEY ARE TOO HARD TO UNDERSTAND

Now, we are getting to something that is much closer to fact than fiction. Part of the reason that the Minor Prophets are so difficult to understand is that their message is so deeply connected to the events of their day. They were reading the daily news, if you will, and speaking the word of the Lord at the same time. And since we don't understand the events of their time, we can't understand their message.

However, it is possible to understand the historical setting of the Minor Prophets. We don't need to have a degree in Old Testament history in order to grasp their history. With the right tools, we can understand the setting of the Minor Prophets.

One of my goals in writing this book is to explain the historical setting of the Minor Prophets so that their message can be heard loud and clear. And I hope to put the cookies on the bottom shelf where people like me can get to them.

So as we turn the page to examine the historical background of the Minor Prophets, please don't skip this chapter.

Please?

# THE HISTORICAL BACKGROUND OF THE MINOR PROPHETS

By now, you may have heard about the incredible Netflix socks, the socks that can detect when you fall asleep while binge watching your favorite Netflix series. The sensors in the socks send a signal to Netflix to pause the show so you won't miss anything important. Who wants to fall asleep with the main character single only to wake up to find her married with two kids? Genius idea, right?

Of course, the devil is in the details. The socks are not actual socks but more like an idea for socks that you can make. Netflix introduced the idea as a "DIY project inspired by you." For these socks to become a part of your life, there are a few necessary steps you must take take. First, go buy a pair of socks. Second, go to an electronics store and purchase about $60 worth of parts including, but not limited to, a micro controller, several infrared LEDs, an accelerometer, and a battery. Don't worry; Netflix will supply the diagram to assemble these tiny electronic parts. You do have a soldering iron, right?

After a little computer programming and sewing the unit into a pair of socks, you are ready to go. If you assembled it correctly, the socks will detect when you have fallen asleep due to the lack of movement and will pause Netflix.

Even if the sock idea doesn't work, binge watching will remain a part of our lives. Thanks to Netflix, we can watch ten seasons worth of a show on one lonely Saturday. And as we wait for season eleven, we can go back and re-watch some of our favorite episodes. Of course, once we have watched the entire season, we can understand each individual episode in its full context.

But imagine if you binge watched a ten season show for the first time in shuffle mode, completely out of order. The events of episode four of season seven would make no sense if you watched them before episode eight of season two. The plot and character development would make no sense. No serious fan would ever do that.

So why do we do that when we try to read the Minor Prophets?

Reading the Minor Prophets can feel like binge watching the Old Testament in shuffle mode. If we don't watch the episodes in order, so to speak, we will be totally confused.

So, let me try to put the episodes in order so that the story of the Minor Prophets makes sense.

I realize that inviting people to a history lesson is like asking for volunteers for a root canal, but if we truly want to become fans of the Minor Prophets, it will be worth the effort. I remind you of the biblical admonition:

> *Do your best to present yourself to God as one approved, a worker who has no need to be ashamed, rightly handling the word of truth. (2 Timothy 2:15 ESV)*

Rightly handling the word of truth does take some effort, but the rewards are better than anything Netflix has to offer.

# THE PREQUEL

More than twenty-five centuries separate today's Bible reader from the world of the Minor Prophets. Since the words of the Lord spoken to and through the Minor Prophets were communicated by real people, living in specific historical contexts to address the particular needs of a certain community, we simply must have at least a basic understanding of the day and times of the Minor Prophets.

God spoke in history and about history, so let's get busy trying to understand that history.

The lives of the Minor Prophets spanned a period of more than three hundred years, from 770 BC to 430 BC. Three hundred and forty years is a long time. The United States of America hasn't even existed for three hundred years. Three hundred years ago, the cities of New Orleans and San Antonio were established by France and Spain, respectively, and the infamous pirate Blackbeard was finally captured. We have gone from the world of pirates and explorers to space travel, constitutions, and cell phones. The world we live in looks nothing like the world of Blackbeard.

But we are not looking backward 300 years, we are trying to understand the history of people who lived on the other side of the world 2700 years ago. The world was different, and yet, in many ways, it was the same.

Before we get to the historical time period of the Minor Prophets, we need to look at the backstory of Israel. Think of this like the prequel to the main story.

The story of the Old Testament really begins in Genesis 12 where God calls Abraham to be the father of a great nation. God promised to give the land of Canaan to the descendants of Abraham. The land of Canaan usually refers to the land west of the Jordan River and the Dead Sea and east of the Mediterranean Sea. It is hard to date the calling of Abraham, but 2000 BC is a good general time stamp.

The story of God's people is then traced through the descendants of Abraham, sons we refer to as the Patriarchs: Isaac, Jacob, and Joseph. Jacob's name was changed to Israel, and he had twelve sons. So when we speak of the "sons of Israel" or the "twelve tribes of Israel," we are linking back to the grandsons of Abraham.

Joseph, one of the children of Jacob (Israel), is the most well-known because his story is told in-depth in the book of Genesis. His brothers sold him into slavery because he told them of the God-given dreams of his future, that his brothers would one day bow down to him. Joseph was sold into slavery in Egypt, and through a dramatic string of events, became the second in command in Egypt. If you are looking for a great short story to read, consider Genesis 37-50 as a great story of betrayal, mystery, surprise, and reconciliation.

The book of Genesis ends with the descendants of Jacob (Israel) moving to live with Joseph in Egypt. Hundreds of years then pass before the book of Exodus begins. In those intervening years, kings of Egypt come and go, and the good contributions of Joseph are forgotten. Instead, the Egyptians had enslaved the descendants of Jacob, now called Hebrews, to use as a slave labor force.

And in that setting, the Lord raised up Moses to deliver His people from slavery in Egypt and to bring them into the Promised Land, the land promised to Abraham.

The first half of the book of Exodus details the dramatic and miraculous ways that God liberated His people. The ten plagues, the Passover meal, and the crossing of the Red Sea are Bible stories that every Bible reader should know. Consider reading Exodus 1-15 as another short story the next time you are sitting in Starbucks and need something to read.

After leaving Egypt around 1440 BC, the children of Israel wandered through the desert for 40 years because they failed to trust the Lord to bring them into the land of promise. But after 40 years of discipline and the death of Moses, the leadership mantle passed to Joshua who led the children of Israel into the land promised to the descendants of Abraham. The book of Joshua tells of the children of Israel conquering the land of promise.

After entering the Promised Land, the children of Israel live in Canaan as a confederation of twelve tribes. As brothers do, sometimes the tribes helped each other and sometimes they fought with each other. But more importantly, the children of Israel repeated a cycle of unfaithfulness for about 400 years. The cycle is described vividly in Judges 2, but the basics are (1) the people began to worship false gods and disobey the commands given to Moses, (2) God used another nation to discipline His people by allowing them to invade the land and subdue it, (3) the people cried out for deliverance, (4) God raised up a judge to deliver the people from the oppressor and to lead them back to faithfulness to the One True God, (5) there was peace in the land as long as the judge was alive, and finally, (6) when the judge died, the people returned to worshipping other gods and disobeying God's commands. Lather, rinse, repeat. The book of Judges describes this period of history as a time when everyone did what was right in their own eyes.

This discouraging cycle was finally broken when the people asked God to give them a king to unite the twelve tribes into one nation. The first king was the disappointing Saul who was crowned around 1050 BC. Saul was then replaced by a man after God's own heart, David. David's son, Solomon, took over the throne and ruled until his death in 921 BC.

After the three kings of the united kingdom of Israel, a major event happened that often confuses Bible readers. At the death of Solomon, the kingdom split into two kingdoms, two nations of God. The northern ten tribes broke away and formed the nation of Israel. The southern two tribes stayed together and formed the nation of Judah. Unfortunately, most of the time, Israel and Judah were at odds with each other, but occasionally they did work together. The books of Samuel, Chronicles, and Kings describe this period of history from Saul through the last king of Judah.

The important thing to remember is that from this time on, there are two nations who are both the people of God. And some Bible stories relate to the nation of Israel, and other Bible stories relate to the nation of Judah. Some prophets were sent to proclaim the word of the Lord to the nation of Israel, and some were sent to the nation of Judah. While both nations were on the same course of unfaithfulness and judgment, it is helpful to keep this fact in mind as we try to understand the Minor Prophets.

This concludes the "prequel" historical period, at least the backstory to the Minor Prophets. During the next 500 plus years, God would send various prophets to both nations to call them back to faithfulness and to warn them of impending judgment should they refuse.

Let's turn the page of history and take a closer look at the days of the Minor Prophet.

# THE NORTHERN KINGDOM OF ISRAEL

The northern nation of Israel was a lost goose from the very beginning. Of the 19 kings of Israel, only one is described in Scripture as "doing what was right in the eyes of the Lord." And throughout their nearly 240 years of existence, the Lord sent prophet after prophet to call them back to faithfulness and to warn them about the impending judgment.

As we examine the message of the Minor Prophets, we will see in great detail why the Lord was so unhappy with Israel (and Judah). However, we can summarize the sin of Israel with these great failures: they turned away from the Lord and worshipped other gods, they disobeyed God's commandments, and they failed to love their neighbor. The prophets in general, and the Minor Prophets specifically, called Israel (and Judah) to confess these sins and return to the Lord.

But after rejecting the word of the Lord, the Lord raised up the nation of Assyria as an instrument of divine judgment. In 722 BC, Assyria not only invaded Israel but functionally wiped them off of the map. Assyria removed some of the citizens of Israel and resettled them elsewhere and then resettled people from other conquered territories in the land of Israel. This region would become known as Samaria. The pure bred Jews of the southern kingdom would think of them as "half breeds" because the remaining Jews of the northern kingdom intermarried with the foreigners settled in that territory. This explains the animosity between the Jews and Samaritans during the days of Jesus, even hundreds of years later.

When trying to understand history, it has always been helpful to me to have a few "stake in the ground dates." These are the firm dates upon which the rest of history hangs. In American history, 1776 (independence from England) and 1865 (end of the civil war) are stakes in the ground to help the student of history arrange other events. Regarding Old Testament history, there are a few "stake in the ground" dates that will help you to arrange the events of the Old Testament.

The first stake in the ground date is 722 BC: the fall of the northern kingdom of Israel to Assyria.

> *The Minor Prophets sent to Israel were Jonah, Amos, and Hosea.*

## THE SOUTHERN KINGDOM OF JUDAH

The southern kingdom of Judah did have some bright spots along their way. Of the twenty kings of Judah, eight are described as righteous. Righteous kings like Josiah, Hezekiah, Asa, Amaziah, and Azariah stand in stark contrast to the evil kings like Ahab and Manasseh. Unfortunately, their story still ended the same. The sin of Judah was the same as the sin of Israel. They turned away from the Lord and worshipped other gods, they disobeyed His commands, and they failed to love their neighbor.

After more than 370 years, and after prophetic warning after prophetic warning, the Lord raised up the nation of Babylon as an instrument of judgment upon the nation of Judah. The invasion of Babylon began in 606 BC and was completed in 586 BC. The nation of Judah fell to Babylon, and Jerusalem was destroyed.

The second significant date to remember is 586 BC: the fall of the southern kingdom of Judah to Babylon.

> *The Minor Prophets sent to Judah were Micah, Zephaniah, Nahum, Habakkuk, and Obadiah.*

## THE EXILE AND RETURN

The fall of Judah was significantly different than the fall of Israel. Whereas Israel ceased to exist as a nation after its defeat to Assyria, the nation of Judah did have a future. Babylon took a large portion of the population of Jerusalem into captivity, forcing them to live in Babylon. This event was prophesied by the prophets to last 70 years. We refer to this event as the Babylonian Exile.

In 538 BC, the nation of Persia defeated Babylon and allowed all the captive peoples to return to their homeland. A remnant returned to the land promised to Abraham. It would take many years to rebuild the city which had been completely destroyed by Babylon. But the remnant rebuilt the city walls in 445 BC and rebuilt the temple in 515 BC.

The third stake in the ground date is 538 BC: the return of the exiles to Jerusalem to rebuild the walls of Jerusalem and the Temple.

> *The Minor Prophets sent to Judah after the exile were Haggai, Zechariah, Joel, and Malachi.*

**Making Sense of It All**

In my eighth grade history class, there was a poster on the wall with this quote: "Those who are ignorant of history are destined to repeat it." I think that was a loose translation of a quote by George Santayana, a Spanish philosopher, but it was Mr. Coker's attempt to motivate a bunch of attention challenged middle school students to study history.

Why should we study history? Because wise people learn from the mistakes of others. We study World War II and the Civil War and the Great Depression because we don't want to repeat those horrible events.

For much of the same reason, we study the history of the life and times of the Minor Prophets so that we don't repeat the same mistakes.

So, what should we learn from this period of biblical history? What did these grumpy old men have to say?

Dr. Todd Pylant

# THE MESSAGE OF THE MINOR PROPHETS

One of the great challenges in the social media world is writing a great Twitter profile. For those who don't know, or don't care, your Twitter profile is your opportunity to introduce yourself to the world in 160 characters. According to Buffer, the "Seven Key Ingredients of a Great Twitter Profile" are:

> *It must be accurate (tell what you really do or who you really are)*
>
> *It must be exciting (make it sound cool)*
>
> *It must be targeted (attract people like yourself)*
>
> *It must be flattering (tell about your accomplishments)*
>
> *It must be humanizing (prove that you are legit)*
>
> *It must be intriguing (invite people to follow you)*
>
> *It must be connected (use hashtags or links)*

Now, that's a hard task to fulfill with 160 characters. And my personal Twitter profile fails at least six of the seven tests. It might accurately state who I really am and what I really do, but it is far from cool and attracting.

What if the Minor Prophets had a Twitter account? What would their Twitter profile look like?

> @minorprophets a voice crying in the wilderness, calling God's people back to covenant faithfulness and warning them of the judgment to come if they don't
>
> @minorprophets twelve grumpy old men who like to point out everyone else's faults
>
> @minorprophets sent by God, with the word of the Lord, calling God's people to repent, sharing the hope of restoration, warning of judgment, looking forward to the messiah
>
> @minorprophets saying what needs to be said even if no one wants to hear it
>
> @minorprophets get off my lawn!

You might come up with something better, but for the Twitter profile to be accurate, it must capture the essential message of the Minor Prophets. But what was that message? While each of the Minor Prophets had a unique message, they did share many common themes.

# MESSAGE #1 - SPIRITUAL ADULTERY

The very first commandment given to Moses was "You shall have no other gods besides me" (Exodus 20.3). The failure to obey this commandment was above all other sins and was the cause of all other sins. The Minor Prophets confronted Israel with their spiritual adultery. The One True God had entered into a covenant with them on Mount Sinai, but the people had been unfaithful to that covenant by worshiping other gods.

If you are looking for an example of spiritual adultery, consider the evil king Manasseh. In 2 Kings 21, the Scriptures detail all the evil he did in the eyes of the

Lord. These included building altars for Baal and Asherah, worshiping the stars, building altars to pagan gods in the Temple itself, burning his sons as an offering to pagan gods, and placing a carved image of Asherah in the house of the Lord. And unfortunately, the people of Judah followed him as he led them to do more evil than the pagan nations who lived in Canaan before Israel entered the land of promise.

So you can see why the prophetic ministry of Hosea was so radical. Hosea was called by God to marry a prostitute to demonstrate that "the land commits great whoredom by forsaking the Lord" (Hosea 1.2 ESV). The prophetic words of Hosea are very clear:

> *My people inquire of a piece of wood, and their walking staff gives them oracles. For a spirit of whoredom has led them astray, and they have left their God to play the whore. They sacrifice on the tops of the mountains and burn offerings on the hills, under oak, poplar, and terebinth, because their shade is good. Therefore your daughters play the whore, and your brides commit adultery. (Hosea 4.12-13 ESV).*

Israel and Judah were guilty of spiritual adultery. In the new covenant, we say that the church is the bride of Christ. In the old covenant, Israel was betrothed to the Lord. To worship other gods was to reject the Lord as their covenantal spouse and to unite with another.

In the New Testament, James uses very similar language as Hosea: "You adulterous people! Do you not know that friendship with the world is enmity with God? Therefore whoever wishes to be a friend of the world makes himself an enemy of God" (James 4:4 ESV). To worship other gods, even the treasures of this world (because greed is idolatry), is to commit spiritual adultery.

So, the Minor Prophets spoke the word of the Lord calling on Israel and Judah to repent of their spiritual adultery and to return to the Lord.

# MESSAGE #2 - HARDENED HEARTS

For over three hundred years, the Minor Prophets called the people of God back to covenantal faithfulness, to stop worshiping false gods, to confess their sins, to obey God's commands, and to treat their neighbor with love and mercy. And for over three hundred years, the people of God refused to repent.

The Hebrew word for repent literally means to "turn around," and some form of this word appears 83 times in the writings of the Minor Prophets.

> *Return, O Israel, to the LORD your God, for you have stumbled because of your iniquity. (Hosea 14.1 ESV)*
>
> *"Yet even now," declares the LORD, "return to me with all your heart, with fasting, with weeping, and with mourning; and rend your hearts and not your garments. Return to the LORD your God, for he is gracious and merciful, slow to anger, and abounding in steadfast love; and he relents over disaster." (Joel 2.12-13 ESV)*
>
> *"I gave you cleanness of teeth in all your cities, and lack of bread in all your places, yet you did not return to me," declares the LORD. (Amos 4.6 ESV)*
>
> *Therefore say to them, Thus declares the LORD of hosts: Return to me, says the LORD of hosts, and I will return to you, says the LORD of hosts. Do not be like your fathers, to whom the former prophets cried out, 'Thus says the LORD of hosts, Return from your evil ways and from your evil deeds.' But they did not hear or pay attention to me, declares the LORD. (Zechariah 1.3-4 ESV)*
>
> *From the days of your fathers you have turned aside from my statutes and have not kept them. Return to me, and I will return to you, says the LORD of hosts. But you say, 'How shall we return?' (Malachi 3.7 ESV)*

There are only four specific examples within the Minor Prophets of a positive response to the call for repentance: Joel 2.12-17, Jonah 3.1-10, Haggai 1.12-14, and Malachi 3.16. But it is remarkable that the most prominent positive response to the preaching of repentance came from the people of Nineveh of Assyria, the Gentile nation used by God to judge Israel. Of course, each of the groups above that did repent relapsed into disobedience, even Assyria (see the book of Nahum).

And there is an interesting interplay with the word "repent" (turn). Because the people of God did not turn towards Him, God would not turn away from pouring out

His judgment. Through the prophets, God graciously called, "Return to me and I will return to you."

But the hearts of His people were hardened, and they refused to repent.

# MESSAGE #3 - INJUSTICE

Reading the Minor Prophets is almost like reading the crime report page of the local newspaper.

> *And I said: Hear, you heads of Jacob and rulers of the house of Israel! Is it not for you to know justice? You who hate the good and love the evil, who tear the skin from off my people and their flesh from off their bones, who eat the flesh of my people, and flay their skin from off them, and break their bones in pieces and chop them up like meat in a pot, like flesh in a cauldron. Then they will cry to the LORD, but he will not answer them; he will hide his face from them at that time, because they have made their deeds evil. (Micah 3.1-4 ESV)*

Micah's words were brutal, and the Minor Prophets were very specific in their accusation of the failure of God's people to work for justice. Crimes of injustice included, but were not limited to...

> *Perverting justice by taking bribes (Amos 5.12)*
>
> *Depriving the poor of justice in the courts (Amos 5.12)*
>
> *Defrauding laborers of their wages (Malachi 3.5)*
>
> *Using the courts to take houses and lands from widows (Micah 2.9)*
>
> *Using false scales to defraud in the marketplace (Amos 8.5)*
>
> *Using slaves and forced labor (Micah 3.10)*

> Using violence to oppress the poor, especially the wealthy and powerful (Micah 6.12)
>
> Mistreating one's family members (Micah 7.6)
>
> Mistreating the foreigner or stranger (Malachi 3.5)

Consider this summary statement from the prophet Zechariah:

> And the word of the LORD came to Zechariah, saying, "Thus says the LORD of hosts, Render true judgments, show kindness and mercy to one another, do not oppress the widow, the fatherless, the sojourner, or the poor, and let none of you devise evil against another in your heart." But they refused to pay attention and turned a stubborn shoulder and stopped their ears that they might not hear. They made their hearts diamond-hard lest they should hear the law and the words that the LORD of hosts had sent by his Spirit through the former prophets. Therefore great anger came from the LORD of hosts. (Zechariah 7.8-12 ESV)

This is why the prophets cried out for "Justice to roll down like waters and righteousness like an ever-flowing stream" (Amos 5.24). The prophets made it clear what God wanted from His people, "To do justice and to love kindness" (Micah 6.8), but the people refused.

The Minor Prophets cried out for justice because those who love God should love others. Jesus connected these two truths when He was asked to identify the greatest commandment.

> "Teacher, which is the great commandment in the Law?" And he said to him, "You shall love the Lord your God with all your heart and with all your soul and with all your mind. This is the great and first commandment. And a second is like it: You shall love your neighbor as yourself. On these two commandments depend all the Law and the Prophets." (Matthew 22.36-40 ESV)

Though we live 2500 years after the ministry of the Minor Prophets, we still hear the voice of our Savior calling us to do justice, to love kindness, and to love our neighbors as ourselves.

# MESSAGE #4 - PERFUNCTORY RELIGION

According to the dictionary, religion is the "service and worship of God." Perfunctory describes actions "characterized by superficiality or routine and lacking in interest or enthusiasm." So, perfunctory religion is religious activity void of genuine devotion to God. It is going through the motions with our body but not engaging the heart. It is outward religious activity without inward love for God. It is all hat and no cattle. It is all show and no go.

In other words, it is pretending to be the people of God.

Perfunctory religion assumes that we are worthy of God's favor. Perfunctory religion assumes that God can be appeased by our religious activity. Perfunctory religion assumes that we can pull a fast one on God, tricking Him into thinking one thing while we actually do another.

But religious activity void of a heart that loves the Lord and obeys His commands is offensive to God, and the Minor Prophets made that very clear.

The word "love" in all its forms appears only 28 times in the Minor Prophets. It ONLY refers to God's love for Israel and NEVER refers to Israel's love for God. Let me say that again, nowhere in the Minor Prophets do we see any evidence that Israel loved God.

Instead, the Minor Prophets confronted Israel with their empty worship. Consider the word of the Lord through the prophet Amos:

> *I hate, I despise your feasts, and I take no delight in your solemn assemblies. Even though you offer me your burnt offerings and grain offerings, I will not accept them; and the peace offerings of your fattened animals, I will not look upon them. Take away from me the noise of your songs; to the melody of your harps I will not listen. (Amos 5.21-23 ESV)*

Or the word of the Lord through Hosea:

> *For I desire steadfast love and not sacrifice, the knowledge of God rather than burnt offerings. (Hosea 6.6 ESV)*

Or the word of the Lord through Malachi:

> *Oh that there were one among you who would shut the doors, that you might not kindle fire on my altar in vain! I have no pleasure in you, says the LORD of hosts, and I will not accept an offering from your hand. (Malachi 1.10 ESV)*

Once again, we see that the message of the Minor Prophets was not confined to Israel and Judah in years gone by. The Minor Prophets continue to call the church to repent of empty worship, of going through the motions with our church attendance but keeping our hearts far from the Lord. The Lord is not honored by our presence in a building on one day of the week. The Lord wants us to love Him with all of our heart, mind, and soul and to obey His commands. He is looking for a people who are seeking after Him with a whole heart.

# MESSAGE #5 - THE DAY OF THE LORD

The coming Day of the Lord is a prominent theme in the Minor Prophets. The exact phrase appears ten times in the Minor Prophets, and variations like "the day" or "that day" or "the day of the Lord's wrath" appear at least thirteen more times.

While new covenant believers instinctively interpret the "Day of the Lord" to refer to the second coming of Jesus, the Minor Prophets used the term to identify events that occurred in their day as well as in the distant future.

> *"The Day of the Lord is both near and far and refers to any time the Lord dramatically intervenes in human history" (Richard Fuhr, The Message of the Twelve, 51).*

For the Minor Prophets, the day of the Lord was the judgment of God upon Israel in the Assyrian conquest, the judgment of God upon Judah in the Babylonian exile, but also the restoration after the exile and the coming Messianic kingdom. In other words, the day of the Lord is both bad news and good news depending on which "day" the prophet was speaking of.

But, most of the time, for the Minor Prophets, the day of the Lord was a "day of darkness and gloom" (Joel 2.2), of "darkness and not light" (Amos 5.18). "The sound of the day of the Lord is bitter" (Zephaniah 1.14). Both Judah and Israel presumed that the Lord would always be on their side, and that the day of the Lord's arrival would always spell victory for them. The Minor Prophets challenged that belief, clarifying that the Day of the Lord was a day of judgment for the enemies of God, of which Israel and Judah had become.

Therefore, most of the time, when the Minor Prophets speak of the day of the Lord, they are warning the people of the impending judgment of God because of their rebellion.

However, the Minor Prophets do speak of "that day" as it refers to the coming Messianic kingdom. In fact, some of the most hopeful descriptions of the Messianic kingdom appear in the Minor Prophets. "That day" will be a day when...

> *The mountains will drip with sweet wine and the hills will flow with milk (Joel 3.18)*
>
> *The fortunes of God's people Israel will be restored (Amos 9.14)*
>
> *The land will be so fruitful that the one who reaps will overtake the one who plants (Amos 9.13)*
>
> *The Lord will reign over them in Jerusalem forevermore (Micah 4.6)*
>
> *The Lord will quiet His people by His love and sing over them (Zephaniah 3.17)*
>
> *There will be peace as nations shall no longer lift up swords against other nations (Micah 4.3)*

When that day comes, there will be peace, there will be prosperity, there will be love because the Messiah will rule the nations from Jerusalem. We owe much of our understanding of the coming kingdom of God to the Minor Prophets.

# MESSAGE #6 - THE COMING MESSIAH

When the magi arrived in Jerusalem looking for the birthplace of the baby Jesus, the priests and the scribes told them that the Christ was to be born in Bethlehem because it was written by the prophet, "And you, O Bethlehem...from you shall come a ruler" (see Matthew 2.1-6).

And who was that prophet? Was it Isaiah or Jeremiah or Ezekiel? No, it was Micah, one of the Minor Prophets. In fact, some of the most important prophecies in the Old Testament about the coming Messiah are found in the Minor Prophets.

> *The future messiah would come from Bethlehem (Micah 5.2)*
>
> *The future messiah would present himself as a man of peace, riding on a donkey (Zechariah 9.9)*
>
> *The people would mourn as they look upon the one whom they have pierced (Zechariah 12.10)*
>
> *The future messiah would sit on the throne as a priest (Zechariah 6.13)*
>
> *The future messiah would shepherd His people in the strength of the Lord (Micah 5.4)*

The Minor Prophets spoke of a coming Messiah who would rule the nations from Jerusalem, who would usher in a true peace, who would reign in justice and righteousness, and who would defeat the enemies of God's people once and for all.

Praise God for sending the Minor Prophets to whet our appetite for the coming messiah!

Dr. Todd Pylant

# THE MESSAGE OF EACH MINOR PROPHET

Although the Minor Prophets share some common themes, each of the Minor Prophets are also unique. They all call the people to confess their sins and repent, and they all warn of judgment should they refuse. However, they each shared that message in a unique way and add more to the conversation.

What follows is a very brief overview of each of the Minor Prophets. This is not meant to give the kind of background that a biblical commentary might give, but it is meant to equip you with enough information to be able to read the prophet in context and to understand the prophet's main message.

Think of what follows as me introducing you to each Minor Prophet as we meet together at a local coffee shop. I'm not trying to tell you their whole story. I'm trying to give you enough of an introduction so that as you chat with the Minor Prophet you will know where they are coming from and what they are talking about. But I will leave it up to you to read their words and hear directly from them.

May I introduce you to…

## HOSEA

Although Hosea is not the first of the Minor Prophets chronologically, Hosea is the first prophet in the Book of the Twelve. This book is unique among the Minor Prophets with its overwhelming imagery of a sordid love story, a living parable of the relationship between God and Israel.

Hosea was called by God to marry a prostitute, Gomer. In this dysfunctional marriage, the rescued bride then abandoned her husband. In the same way, God had rescued Israel, and she had become His bride. But Israel had become unfaithful, turning to other gods.

This marriage metaphor was only one family image used in Hosea to illustrate Israel's rebellion against the Lord. Israel was not only an unfaithful wife, but also an indifferent mother, an illegitimate child, an ungrateful son, a stubborn heifer, and a silly dove.

The primary accusation against Israel is their worship of Baal and participation in the immoral cult prostitution at the pagan temples: "For the men themselves go aside with prostitutes and sacrifice with cult prostitutes" (Hosea 4.14 ESV). Like Hosea, God had married an unfaithful wife.

The names of Hosea's children tell the prophetic story. The first child was named "Jezreel" foretelling that God would bring an end to the kingdom of Israel. The second child was named "No Mercy" indicating that God would no longer have mercy on Israel. The third child was named "Not My People" declaring that Israel was not His people and He was not their God. The result is that Israel would "go up from the land" (Hosea 1.11 ESV). Israel had sowed the wind, and they would reap the whirlwind (see Hosea 8.7).

Hosea's ministry focused on the northern kingdom of Israel, though he did speak much about the southern kingdom of Judah. He prophesied for a period of 30 years around the fall of Israel to Assyria in 722 BC.

The apostle Peter picks up the words of Hosea to describe the covenant people of God who were made righteous by grace through faith:

> *But you are a chosen race, a royal priesthood, a holy nation, a people for his own possession, that you may proclaim the excellencies of him who called you out of darkness into his marvelous light. Once you were not a people, but now you are God's people; once you had not received mercy, but now you have received mercy. (1 Peter 2.9-10 ESV)*

By God's grace, sinners like me, who were once not part of God's family, have received mercy and have become members of God's household. And as part of God's family, the prophet Hosea continues to call the people of God to live as the pure bride of Christ.

The Book of Twelve begins with this shocking story of gross immorality and unfaithfulness. The reader is now called to step deeper into the world of the Minor Prophets.

# JOEL

The prophet Joel is not mentioned elsewhere in the Old Testament, and there are few internal clues as to when he lived and where he ministered. Most scholars believe that Joel ministered after the exile because the exile was treated as a past event (Joel 3.2-3), the conquest of Jerusalem was mentioned (Joel 3.17), no king was mentioned in the book, and the temple played a prominent role. Though a date cannot be certain, some have suggested that Joel prophesied around 500 BC, after the Temple had been rebuilt in Jerusalem.

The book begins with a national disaster, a locust plague. Whether the plague is literal or figurative of an invading army, the prophet calls the people to repent before even more destruction comes from the Lord. Unlike in previous times, the people responded to the words of the prophet and repent. As a result, the Lord promised to repay His people for the years the locusts had eaten (Joel 2.25).

The message of Joel does not require an exact date or setting to encourage the people of God. When God convicts of sin and His people confess and repent, He has promised to forgive.

> *If we confess our sins, he is faithful and just to forgive us our sins and to cleanse us from all unrighteousness. (1 John 1.9 ESV)*

The apostle Peter quoted from Joel on the Day of Pentecost after the resurrection of Jesus to explain the gift of the Holy Spirit to a confused crowd.

> *But this is what was uttered through the prophet Joel: "And in the last days it shall be, God declares, that I will pour out my Spirit on all flesh, and your sons and your daughters shall prophesy, and your young men shall see visions, and your old men shall dream dreams; even on my male servants and female servants in those days I will pour out my Spirit, and they shall prophesy." (Acts 2.16-18 ESV)*

Joel points believers to the promise of forgiveness and the gift of the Spirit.

# AMOS

The prophet Amos lived during a time of unprecedented prosperity for the wealthy class of Israel. Unfortunately, the majority of people lived in poverty and were oppressed by the wealthy. Therefore, Amos preached about the justice of God. Social justice is a primary theme in this book.

The prophet was a skilled communicator, even though he identified himself as just a shepherd and a fruit picker. To lead Israel to see their own sin, he condemned the injustices of Israel's enemies. And as they were shouting "Amen," he aimed his words at the home crowd. Israel was worthy of God's wrath because they "trampled the head of the poor" (Amos 2.7 ESV). The prophet constantly called the people to "hate evil, and love good, and establish justice in the gates" (Amos 5.15 ESV).

The most well-known words of Amos, once quoted by Martin Luther King, Jr. in his famous "I Have A Dream" speech, are:

> *But let justice roll down like waters, and righteousness like an ever-flowing stream. (Amos 5.24 ESV)*

Amos is filled with words of judgment against the mistreatment of the poor by the rich, but it is also filled with a condemnation of their perfunctory religiosity. The prophet essentially said, "Why don't you go to church and sin?" (see Amos 4.4). God so disliked their worship that He pleaded for someone to "take away from me the noise of your songs" (Amos 5.23 ESV).

In the New Testament, James echoes the same concern of Amos when he wrote:

> *My brothers, show no partiality as you hold the faith in our Lord Jesus Christ, the Lord of glory. For if a man wearing a gold ring and fine clothing comes into your assembly, and a poor man in shabby clothing also comes in, and if you pay attention to the one who wears the fine clothing and say, "You sit here in a good place," while you say to the poor man, "You stand over there," or, "Sit down at my feet," have you not then made distinctions among yourselves and become judges with evil thoughts? Listen, my beloved brothers, has not God chosen those who are poor in the world to be rich in faith and heirs of the kingdom, which he has promised to those who love him? But you have dishonored the poor man. Are not the rich the ones who oppress you,*

> *and the ones who drag you into court? Are they not the ones who blaspheme the honorable name by which you were called? If you really fulfill the royal law according to the Scripture, "You shall love your neighbor as yourself," you are doing well. But if you show partiality, you are committing sin and are convicted by the law as transgressors. (James 2.1-9 ESV)*

The prophet Amos calls the people of God to love justice just as the Lord loves justice.

# OBADIAH

There is nothing quite as brutal and cruel as family rivalry, particularly when hatred arises between brothers. The prophet Obadiah preached about the conflict between the descendants of Jacob (Judah) and his brother Esau (Edom). In the twenty-one verses, the shortest book in the Old Testament, the prophet declares the word of the Lord that God would destroy Edom for their violence against Judah and that He would ultimately restore Israel.

The name Obadiah means "servant of the Lord," and was a common name in the Old Testament. In fact, twelve other individuals in the biblical narrative share that name. This Obadiah ministered between the fall of Jerusalem in 586 BC and the fall of Edom in 533 BC.

The reason for the prophecy is that during the siege of Jerusalem by Babylon, Edom took advantage and joined in the pillaging of Jerusalem.

> *Because of the violence done to your brother Jacob, shame shall cover you, and you shall be cut off forever. On the day that you stood aloof, on the day that strangers carried off his wealth and foreigners entered his gates and cast lots for Jerusalem, you were like one of them. But do not gloat over the day of your brother in the day of his misfortune; do not rejoice over the people of Judah in the day of their ruin; do not boast in the day of distress. (Obadiah 1.10-12 ESV)*

The short book ends with a warning for Edom: "As you have done, it shall be done to you" (Obadiah 15) and "there shall be no survivors for the house of Esau" (Obadiah 18).

The prophet Obadiah calls the people of God to refuse to rejoice in the misfortune of our enemies but to love our enemies as Jesus commanded.

# JONAH

Jonah is by far the most well-known of the twelve Minor Prophets. The prophet first shows up in 2 Kings where he prophesied that the Lord would expand the borders of Israel (see 2 Kings 14.23-27). I am pretty sure that made him well-liked in Israel, but his next assignment would be much harder than preaching to the choir.

Sometime between 793 and 753 BC, the Lord called Jonah to go to Nineveh, a significant city in the dreaded nation of Assyria. He was to call them to repent. As the story unfolds, we discover that the prophet did not want to obey because he feared the people would repent and the Lord would show them mercy. Jonah wanted Nineveh to suffer the wrath of God. He wanted Israel alone to have a monopoly on the mercy of God.

Jonah's attempt to run away from the Lord was unsuccessful. The Lord caught up to his getaway ship with a storm, and Jonah was tossed overboard. A great fish was appointed by God to swallow Jonah, and for three days, the prophet had time to confess and repent of his disobedience. The Lord then commanded the fish to vomit Jonah onto dry land, and then He issued the call once again. This time, Jonah obeyed.

He preached a simple message: "Yet forty days, and Nineveh shall be overthrown" (Jonah 3.4 ESV). The sermon was short but effective, for the people repented of their sins, and the Lord relented from the planned disaster. This displeased the prophet which caused the Lord to ask the prophet, "Should I not pity Nineveh, that great city, in which there are more than 120,000 persons who do not know their right hand from their left?" (Jonah 4.11 ESV).

The book leaves that question hanging. We don't know how Jonah answered the Lord's question. But more importantly, the question still challenges the people of God today? Do we want others to know and experience the mercy of God? Do we want our enemies to know God's favor, or do we want exclusive rights to the mercy of God?

Of course, the legacy of Jonah extends far beyond the question of God's mercy to our enemies. The three days in the belly of the fish were a sign of the death and burial of the Lord Jesus.

> *But he answered them, "An evil and adulterous generation seeks for a sign, but no sign will be given to it except the sign of the prophet Jonah. For just as Jonah was three days and three nights in the belly of the great fish, so will the Son of Man be three days and three nights in the heart of the earth. The men of Nineveh will rise up at the judgment with this generation and condemn it, for they repented at the preaching of Jonah, and behold, something greater than Jonah is here." (Matthew 12.39-41 ESV)*

# MICAH

The prophet Micah's name means, "Who is like the Lord," and the book ends with that exact same question, "Who is a God like you?" (Micah 7.18 ESV). Micah ministered to the southern kingdom of Judah during and after the fall of the northern kingdom to Assyria. Though Judah did not fall to Assyria like their northern neighbors, they almost did. In fact, Assyria surrounded Jerusalem and their defeat was inevitable. You may remember the story of the prophet Isaiah calling Hezekiah the king to trust in the Lord to deliver Jerusalem, but Micah was also credited with speaking to Hezekiah and leading him to faith.

Many years later, when the prophet Jeremiah was in trouble with the religious leaders for his prophetic words, some of the priests remembered the prophetic words of Micah and how the king treated that prophet:

> *Then the officials and all the people said to the priests and the prophets, "This man does not deserve the sentence of death, for he has spoken to us in the name of the LORD our God." And certain of the elders of the land arose and spoke to all the assembled people, saying, "Micah of Moresheth prophesied in the days of Hezekiah king of Judah, and said to all the people of Judah: 'Thus says the LORD of hosts, "'Zion shall be plowed as a field; Jerusalem shall become a heap of ruins, and the mountain of the house a wooded height.' Did Hezekiah king of Judah and all Judah put him to death? Did he not fear the LORD and entreat the favor of the LORD, and did not the LORD relent of the disaster that*

> he had pronounced against them? But we are about to bring great disaster upon ourselves." (Jeremiah 26.16-19 ESV)

This story from the life of Jeremiah demonstrates that the warnings of Micah were headed by the King of Judah at least for a little while.

Micah was a contemporary of Isaiah, and their prophesies mirrored each other in several ways: they both warned of a future exile in Babylon, they both promised deliverance from Assyria, they both prophesied that the Lord would raise up a son from the line of David to rule His people, they both anticipated the exiles would return from Assyria and Babylon, and they both spoke of Zion as the highest mountain on the earth in the coming messianic kingdom. In fact, the similarities between Isaiah 2.2-4 and Micah 4.1-5 are so striking that many scholars wonder if one copied from the other.

The prophetic work of Micah is structured into three major sections, each issuing a warning of judgment followed by a promise of restoration and salvation. The Judge who scatters His people is also the Good Shepherd who gathers them back together and forgives them.

As the prophet calls the people of God to repent, he makes known what God wants from His people:

> He has told you, O man, what is good; and what does the LORD require of you but to do justice, and to love kindness, and to walk humbly with your God? (Micah 6.8 ESV)

The prophet Micah continues to call the people of God to do justice, to love kindness, and to walk in humble obedience to our God.

# NAHUM

The preaching of Jonah was effective, but not long lasting. The repentance of Nineveh was short lived, and they soon returned to their evil ways. As a result, God gave the prophet Nahum an oracle about the coming judgment of Assyria. Nahum shared this oracle during the height of the Assyrian Empire, when the fall of this powerful nation would have been inconceivable. As the Lord said through Nahum,

"Though they are at full strength and many, they will be cut down and pass away" (Nahum 1.12 ESV).

This prophecy was fulfilled in 612 BC when Assyria fell to the Babylonians.

As the prophet's name means, this prophecy was meant to bring comfort to the people of God.

The prophet Nahum reminds us that the Lord is the God of the nations and will judge all peoples in righteousness.

# HABAKKUK

This prophet should be called the Minor Psalmist rather than a Minor Prophet. His work is not so much a word from the Lord to share with the people. Instead, his work is a conversation between the prophet and God. It reads like a journal or prayer book. Not only does the work resonate with common themes from the Psalms, but chapter three is an actual psalm, written by the prophet.

Over and over, the psalmists wrestle with the question of why the righteous suffer while the evil prosper.

> *Behold, these are the wicked; always at ease, they increase in riches. (Psalm 73.12 ESV)*

In the same way, Habakkuk wrestled with this very question.

> *"O Lord, how long shall I cry for help and you will not hear...for the wicked surround the righteous and justice goes forth perverted." (see Habakkuk 1.1-4 ESV)*

The prophet talked with God about this issue most likely between the religious reforms of King Josiah (622 BC) and the final fall of Jerusalem (586 BC). Judah had turned against the Lord and injustice and wickedness reigned in the land. So, the prophet asked the question, "God, why aren't you going to do something about this?" God answered the prophet by sharing His plan to use Babylon as an instrument of His judgment. To which the prophet cried out, "But how can you use them to judge Judah? They are worse than we are!"

Habakkuk is one of the most practical of all the Minor Prophets as the prophet wrestled with one of the most basic struggles of mankind: the problem of evil. Habakkuk was called to trust in God's plan and in God's timing.

The key phrase in this book is "the righteous shall live by his faith" (Habakkuk 2.4 ESV) which is quoted three times in the New Testament (Romans 1.17, Galatians 3.11, Hebrews 10.38).

The prophet calls believers to put their faith in God and to trust Him to judge evil doers in His time and in His way.

# ZEPHANIAH

A common summary of the Minor Prophets goes something like this: "Things are going to get really, really bad and then things are going to get really, really good." Not all of the prophets fit this simple template of a warning of judgment and then the promise of restoration, but Zephaniah does.

> *In three chapters, it offers the bread and butter of the writing prophets: announcements of judgment, a call to repentance, and promises of salvation (Richard Fuhr, Message of the Prophets, 237).*

Zephaniah prophesied during the days of Josiah, one of the righteous kings of Judah. After his father had led the nation into gross idolatry and immorality, Josiah tried to lead the nation back to covenantal faithfulness. Unfortunately, his reforms did not last after his death. The word of the Lord through Zephaniah was very clear: "I will stretch out my hand against Judah and against all the inhabitants of Jerusalem" (Zephaniah 1.4 ESV).

Zephaniah spoke repeatedly about the day of the Lord, more than any other Minor Prophet. And he used it both to describe the coming judgment and wrath expressed through the Babylonian exile (Zephaniah 1.14) and the promise of restoration (Zephaniah 3.16).

The prophet calls believers not only to repent of their sin before a holy God but also to rest in God's promises of restoration for the faithful remnant of His people.

# HAGGAI

By now, the history behind the Minor Prophets should be clear. Jerusalem fell to Babylon in 586 BC and the Temple was destroyed. Babylon fell to Persia in 539 BC, and the captives were allowed to return to Jerusalem. In 537 BC, thousands of Jews returned to Jerusalem, built an altar on the ruins of the Temple, and celebrated the Festival of Booths. Later the next year, they laid the foundation for the Temple. But as the historical books of Ezra and Nehemiah describe, the Jews encountered great opposition to their efforts to rebuild the Temple. By 520 BC, the work had stopped entirely.

The book of Haggai is a collection of four oracles delivered by the prophet over a four month period in 520 BC, between August and December. Unlike other Minor Prophets, this book is very exact in the dating of Haggai's prophecies. The main message was to encourage the people of God to rebuild the Temple and to remain faithful in the worship of the One True God.

The prophet chastised them for working hard to build their own homes but neglecting the house of the Lord (see Haggai 1.4). The prophet encouraged them that the "latter glory of this house shall be greater than the former" (Haggai 2.9 ESV). These four sermons, captured in only three chapters, were very effective. The people responded, completing the rebuilt Temple in 515 BC.

Haggai calls believers to work hard for the Lord, yet through the power of His Spirit who remains in our midst (see Haggai 2.5).

# ZECHARIAH

When the Jews returned to Jerusalem after the exile, life among the ruins was not easy. The people heard the prophets speak of restoration, but they were not experiencing the fullness of promised blessings. Zechariah prophesied during these hard times, during the days of "the now but not yet." As he preached alongside Haggai, he too called the people to finish the Temple in the power of the Lord. But Zechariah lifted up their eyes to see the future messianic kingdom when the people of God would know and experience the full restoration.

The book has two distinct sections: chapters 1-8 and chapters 9-14. In the first section, the prophet received eight night visions that promise the Lord's blessings on the rebuilding of Jerusalem.

The second section deals more with future events, some even future to believers today. These chapters contain some of the greatest visions of the coming messiah, the coming kingdom of God, and the eternity we all long for. As a result, the New Testament writers either quote directly or allude to 54 passages from Zechariah in about 67 different places in the New Testament. The verses most directly quoted are Zechariah 8.16 (Ephesians 4.25), Zechariah 9.9 (Matthew 21.5 and John 12.15), Zechariah 11.12-13 (Matthew 27.9-10), Zechariah 12.10 (John 19.37), and Zechariah 13.7 (Matthew 26.31 and Mark 14.27).

Many of the prophecies in the second section are hard to understand. It can be difficult to discern whether the prophet was speaking of the restoration of Jerusalem, the first coming of the Messiah, or the second coming of the Messiah. But many of our Christological hopes are rooted in Zechariah's prophecies:

> *Rejoice greatly, O daughter of Zion! Shout aloud, O daughter of Jerusalem! Behold, your king is coming to you; righteous and having salvation is he, humble and mounted on a donkey, on a colt, the foal of a donkey. (Zechariah 9.9 ESV)*

> *And I will pour out on the house of David and the inhabitants of Jerusalem a spirit of grace and pleas for mercy, so that, when they look on me, on him whom they have pierced, they shall mourn for him, as one mourns for an only child, and weep bitterly over him, as one weeps over a firstborn. (Zechariah 12.10 ESV)*

> *And the LORD will be king over all the earth. On that day the LORD will be one and his name one. (Zechariah 14.9 ESV)*

The prophet Zechariah calls believers to keep looking forward to the coming day of the Lord as we live in the "now and the not yet." There are blessings in the Lord today, but the full restoration is yet to come.

# MALACHI

The last Minor Prophet, and the last book in the Old Testament, is Malachi. Unfortunately, many believers only know Malachi as a call to "bring the full tithe" (Malachi 3.10 ESV). But to reduce this book to a stewardship sermon is to miss the point completely.

Malachi ministers in the same period as Haggai, Zechariah, Ezra, and Nehemiah. The people of God have returned to Jerusalem. And while they are no longer involved in active idolatry, their worship of God had become perfunctory. They are not following the Lord's commands but are still wondering why the Lord was not blessing them. Like Habakkuk, the book of Malachi reads like a back and forth conversation between God and the people of Israel.

The issues in Malachi are as contemporary to modern day Christianity as is much of the New Testament. The prophet continues to call the people to love God with their hearts and not just in empty religious activity. The prophet calls the religious leaders to speak only the truth to the people and not to cause anyone to stumble. The prophet calls the people to honor their marriage vows instead of seeking divorce. The prophet calls the people to give unto God what belongs to Him, including their finances. All of these issues, and more, are relevant issues to believers today.

The book, and the entire Old Testament, ends with a prophesy of God sending Elijah before the great and awesome day of the Lord comes (see Malachi 4.5). Jesus identified John the Baptist as the Elijah who was to come (see Matthew 11.13-14).

The prophet Malachi calls believers today to worship the Lord with all of our heart and challenges us to fully obey the commands of Jesus.

# HOW TO READ THE MINOR PROPHETS

The Bible promises us that the Minor Prophets are profitable to read. God will use them to teach us truth, convict us of our sins, train us in righteousness, and equip us for the good work He has created us to do. However, there is no denying the reality that the Minor Prophets are some of the hardest books of the Bible to both understand and to make profitable. Discovering the original meaning of the prophet to his historical context and then converting that message to our lives can be challenging, but there are a few basic principles that can help us along the way.

## 1. UNDERSTAND THEIR HISTORICAL SETTING

By this point in the book, I hope I have impressed upon you the importance of knowing the historical setting of the Minor Prophets. God spoke in history and to history, so we must work to understand the historical setting of each Minor Prophet as we read them. Basically, the historical setting of each Minor Prophet can be summarized into one of the three time periods:

> *Some of the the Minor Prophets spoke to the nation of Israel warning them of the judgment of God in the form of the Assyrian invasion (Jonah, Amos, and Hosea).*

> *Some of the Minor Prophets spoke to the nation of Judah warning them of the judgment of God in the form of the Babylonian exile (Micah, Zephaniah, Nahum, Habakkuk, and Obadiah).*
>
> *Some of the Minor Prophets spoke to the Jews who had returned to Jerusalem after the exile to rebuild Jerusalem and the temple (Haggai, Zechariah, Joel, and Malachi).*

It is incumbent upon Bible readers to have a working knowledge of the basic historical events surrounding Israel and Judah between 800 and 400 BC.

## 2. UNDERSTAND THEIR ORIGINAL MESSAGE

Bible readers today often want to jump immediately into application when reading the Bible. Too quickly we ask, "What does this mean for me today?" But we cannot clearly know the answer to that question unless we have already asked, "What did this mean for the original hearers?" What was God trying to communicate through Hosea to the people who lived in Israel over 2700 years ago? Only by having a strong grasp on that message can we begin to apply the Minor Prophets to our own lives.

The Minor Prophets were primarily doing three things:

First, the Minor Prophets were condemning Israel and Judah for their sins of worshiping other gods, disobeying the commands given to Moses, stubbornly refusing to repent and to return to God, perverting justice, failing to love others, and pretending to be religious while living in rebellion to the Lord.

Second, the Minor Prophets were warning the people of the impending judgment of God should they continue to walk in rebellion.

Third, the Minor Prophets spoke of the hope of restoration when the people did repent and of the ultimate hope of restoration with the coming of the messiah.

Before we apply these words to our lives, we must have a good grasp on what it meant to those who heard Micah or Joel preach for the first time.

# 3. UNDERSTAND THE DIFFERENCE BETWEEN THE OLD AND NEW COVENANT

The next step is to make sure that we read the words of the Minor Prophets in light of the new covenant and understand what that does and does not mean.

**The New Way of the Spirit**

The old covenant of law was different than the new covenant of grace (praise the Lord!). In the old covenant, the people of God lived in a right relationship with God by obeying His commandments. These commands included moral commands but also dietary restrictions, cleanliness codes, Sabbath rules, and other ceremonial instructions. And when they failed to obey them all, which they did regularly, they were to seek forgiveness through the sacrificial system.

But the old covenant was weak in that it was never able to take away sin. Through obedience to the law, men and women were never able to find freedom from their sin nature and were never able to fulfill the righteous requirements of the law.

> *For by works of the law no human being will be justified in his sight, since through the law comes knowledge of sin. (Romans 3.20 ESV)*

But Christ has set us free from the law and accomplished what the law never could, to fulfill the righteous requirement of the law in us.

> *For God has done what the law, weakened by the flesh, could not do. By sending his own Son in the likeness of sinful flesh and for sin, he condemned sin in the flesh, in order that the righteous requirement of the law might be fulfilled in us, who walk not according to the flesh but according to the Spirit. (Romans 8.3-4 ESV)*

As a result, those in the new covenant are now in the age of grace and truth, and we serve God through the new way of the Spirit.

> *But now we are released from the law, having died to that which held us captive, so that we serve in the new way of the Spirit and not in the old way of the written code. (Romans 7.6 ESV)*

Salvation by faith in Christ's atoning death and sanctification by the ongoing work of the Holy Spirit is a radical departure from the old covenant. We are made right with God by His grace as a gift through the redemption that is in Christ Jesus.

> *But now the righteousness of God has been manifested apart from the law, although the Law and the Prophets bear witness to it--the righteousness of God through faith in Jesus Christ for all who believe. For there is no distinction: for all have sinned and fall short of the glory of God, and are justified by his grace as a gift, through the redemption that is in Christ Jesus. (Romans 3.21-24 ESV)*

Does that mean that believers in the new covenant are set free from obeying God's commands? Absolutely not! It does mean that we obey God's commands not to earn His favor but because we have already received His favor. And it means that we are empowered to obey His commands through His Spirit. As we walk in the Spirit, we will not carry out the desires of the flesh.

> *But I say, walk by the Spirit, and you will not gratify the desires of the flesh. (Galatians 5.16 ESV)*

The old covenant points toward Christ as the once and for all sacrifice for our sins (see Hebrews 7.27). God's wrath for our sin has been satisfied. However, God's passion for holiness is alive and well. The New Testament is very clear that God disciplines the children whom He loves (see Hebrews 12.3-11), and it is a terrifying thing to fall into the hands of the living God.

We cannot simply dismiss the warnings of the Minor Prophets as words to poor old Israel. We must hear the warnings of the Minor Prophets, the warnings of judgment should we fail to repent, with just as much conviction as Israel and Judah should have heard them in the first place. Consider the words of the New Testament writer of Hebrews:

> *Anyone who has set aside the law of Moses dies without mercy on the evidence of two or three witnesses. How much worse punishment, do you think, will be deserved by the one who has trampled underfoot the Son of God, and has profaned the blood of the covenant by which he was sanctified, and has outraged the Spirit of grace? For we know him who said, "Vengeance is mine; I will repay." And again, "The Lord will judge his people." It is a fearful thing to fall into the hands of the living God. (Hebrews 10.28-31 ESV)*

According to the writer of Hebrews, those who trample underfoot the Son of God are actually under worse punishment than those of the old covenant who set aside the law of Moses. This means that we should read the words of the Minor Prophets with even greater attention, not less.

God is still a holy God, and He still judges His people when they rebel against Him.

**The Kingdom of God**

Beyond the means of justification, one other major difference between the old and new covenants is that the old covenant was geographically and ethnically limited to Israel. God entered into the old covenant with the Twelve Tribes of Israel, a very specific lineage of people. Only those who were physical descendants of Abraham were part of the chosen people of God.

But in the new covenant, all those of faith are descendants of Abraham (see Galatians 3.7). Gentile believers have been grafted into Israel (see Romans 11.17-24). All who believe can become children of God (see John 1.12). Therefore, as we read the Minor Prophets, we know that God's vision for the kingdom is that believers from all nations and peoples and languages will surround the throne.

In the new covenant of grace, the kingdom of God is not limited to the geographical nation of Israel. Again, all nations and peoples are welcome to the wedding banquet by grace through faith. So, as we read the Minor Prophets, we can hear God's love for Israel as it extends to all nations and all peoples.

In fact, the eternal hope of restoration is that the world will be united in peace, peacefully ruled by the righteous and merciful messiah. So as we read the Minor Prophets and hear God's promises to rebuild Jerusalem, new covenant believers are pointed towards God's promise to rebuild the heavens and the earth for believers from all nations, tribes, people groups, and languages.

# 4. LISTEN FOR GOD TO CONTINUE TO SPEAK

So far, we have talked about knowing the historical setting of the Minor Prophets, understanding what they were trying to communicate to the original hearers, and the distinction between the old and new covenants. But, if we are not careful, we can begin to treat the Minor Prophets like a scholarly work that can only be analyzed by Bible scholars.

But we must reject the idea that reading the Minor Prophets is a purely academic exercise. We can and should read the Minor Prophets devotionally. The devotional reading of the Bible means to read the Bible with the expectation of hearing God speak to us personally in ways that apply to our life and relationship with Christ.

And this certainly applies to the Minor Prophets.

The Minor Prophets teach us truth about God's steadfast love, about His holiness, and about His divine eternal plan. The Minor Prophets convict us of the sin of perfunctory worship, injustice, and greed. The Minor Prophets train us in the righteousness of God. The Minor Prophets equip us to be ambassadors for Christ. We neglect the Minor Prophets to our own peril.

So, I want to encourage you to include the Minor Prophets in your daily Bible reading plan. A good, lifelong Bible reading plan will include regular readings from the gospels, the New Testament letters, the Psalms and Proverbs, the historical books of the Old Testament, and the prophets, including the Minor Prophets. We should read the Minor Prophets expecting that God will teach, correct, and train us in righteousness.

As you read the Minor Prophets, look for that verse or verses that "leap off the page" that the Holy Spirit is drawing your attention to. Then take a few moments to understand the verse in its context, but be sure to ask the question, "Lord, what are you saying to me? How can I learn to praise you from the Minor Prophets? How are you convicting me of my sin through the Minor Prophets? How are you teaching me to pray through the Minor Prophets?"

# 5. LOOK FOR THE DEPTH OF GOD'S WRATH

When we read the Minor Prophets, we should not too quickly dismiss the warnings of impending judgment nor the condemnation of sin. True, those warnings and condemnations were spoken to the people in Israel and Judah hundreds of years ago, but the believer should hear God's passion for holiness and justice and obedience. We should hear how much God's hates idolatry. We should hear how much God hates injustice. We should hear how much God hates the mistreatment of one's neighbor. We should hear how much God hates empty religion. And God's hatred for evil should call His people to seek holiness and righteousness.

> *For the wrath of God is revealed from heaven against all ungodliness and unrighteousness of men, who by their unrighteousness suppress the truth. (Romans 1.18 ESV)*

Further, as we see God's horrible punishment for sin, especially the destruction of Jerusalem and the exile into Babylon, we should learn something about the "wages of sin." While we see sin as no big deal or just a personal struggle to better ourselves, God sees sin as an affront to His holiness and rebellion. His judgment upon sin is His wrath, and eventually, that wrath will settle eternally on the unholy stain of sin.

> *Put to death therefore what is earthly in you: sexual immorality, impurity, passion, evil desire, and covetousness, which is idolatry. On account of these the wrath of God is coming. (Colossians 3.5-6 ESV)*

The Minor Prophets focus our attention on the judgment of God in the fall of Jerusalem. The destruction was total. The exile was horrifying. The wrath of God poured out upon His people was fearful. But that wrath was only a shadow of the wrath of God yet to come. The wrath of God upon sin revealed in the final judgment will be far greater. And as we see the shadow of God's wrath to come in the Minor Prophets, we see the depth of God's grace in our salvation.

Reading the Minor Prophets should call believers to see the glory of the Cross and the depth of our salvation. We have been redeemed from the wrath of God! We have been redeemed from the justly deserved consequences of our sin as a grace gift! Oh, what destruction God has rescued us from!

> *Wait for his Son from heaven, whom he raised from the dead, Jesus who delivers us from the wrath to come. (1 Thessalonians 1.10 ESV)*

Praise God for the Minor Prophets as they help us to see the depth of God's wrath so that we can delight in the depth of His grace.

# 6. LOOK FOR THE DEPTH OF GOD'S STEADFAST LOVE

The Minor Prophets are much more than just grumpy old men who always pointed out the sin of God's people and warned of impending judgment. They also demonstrated the great depths of God's steadfast love.

The Hebrew word *hessed* is often translated as "steadfast love," and it is this great Old Testament word that describes God's favor, faithfulness, kindness, loyalty, mercy, and unchanging love. And some of the most meaningful expressions of that steadfast love can be found among the words of the Minor Prophets.

For example, remember that God called Hosea to marry an unfaithful woman to demonstrate Israel's unfaithfulness to the Lord. The name of Hosea's children proclaimed God's wrath upon the people who had committed spiritual adultery against Him. He was to name his children "Not My People" and "No Mercy."

But even after two chapters of the prophetic words of condemnation and judgment, the steadfast love of the Lord comes shining through. The Lord says to unfaithful Israel that a day is coming where the relationship will be restored:

> *And I will betroth you to me forever. I will betroth you to me in righteousness and in justice, in steadfast love and in mercy. I will betroth you to me in faithfulness. And you shall know the LORD. And in that day I will answer, declares the LORD, I will answer the heavens, and they shall answer the earth, and the earth shall answer the grain, the wine, and the oil, and they shall answer Jezreel, and I will sow her for myself in the land. And I will have mercy on No Mercy, and I will say to Not My People, 'You are my people'; and he shall say, 'You are my God.'" (Hosea 2.19-23 ESV)*

The apostle Peter meditated on this redemptive work of God. In light of the wrath of God justly earned for our sins, listen to how Peter expressed the grace of God in the language of the Minor Prophets:

> *But you are a chosen race, a royal priesthood, a holy nation, a people for his own possession, that you may proclaim the excellencies of him who called you out of darkness into his marvelous light. Once you were not a*

> *people, but now you are God's people; once you had not received mercy, but now you have received mercy. (1 Peter 2.9-10 ESV)*

Once, we were "Not My People," but through Christ, we now are God's people. Once, we were called "No Mercy," but now we have received mercy in Christ.

What depths of love the Lord has for faithless Israel, and for sinners like myself. And the Minor Prophets demonstrate this steadfast love in ways that no other book in the Bible can do. And so, we need to read the Minor Prophets to see and feel the depth of God's steadfast love for us.

# 7. LOOK FOR THE HOPE OF THE MESSIAH

Finally, we should read the Minor Prophets to see the incredible description of the coming Kingdom of God. As we have already noted, the Minor Prophets contain some of the greatest descriptions of the coming Kingdom of God in all the Bible. To see the gross injustice in wicked Israel and then to dream of the just society of the messianic kingdom is to breathe in the beauty of God's plan for eternity. To see the broken reality of Israel and to dream of the peace of the messianic kingdom generates anticipation for the kingdom.

Allow me to remind you of just some of the glory of the eternal kingdom of God described in the Minor Prophets:

> *But you, O Bethlehem Ephrathah, who are too little to be among the clans of Judah, from you shall come forth for me one who is to be ruler in Israel, whose coming forth is from of old, from ancient days. Therefore he shall give them up until the time when she who is in labor has given birth; then the rest of his brothers shall return to the people of Israel. And he shall stand and shepherd his flock in the strength of the LORD, in the majesty of the name of the LORD his God. And they shall dwell secure, for now he shall be great to the ends of the earth. And he shall be their peace. (Micah 5.2-5 ESV)*

Under the messianic ruler, whose coming forth is from of old, the people of God will live under the care and majesty of the Good Shepherd. We will be secure and will finally know true and lasting peace.

> *"Behold, the days are coming," declares the LORD, "when the plowman shall overtake the reaper and the treader of grapes him who sows the seed; the mountains shall drip sweet wine, and all the hills shall flow with it. I will restore the fortunes of my people Israel, and they shall rebuild the ruined cities and inhabit them; they shall plant vineyards and drink their wine, and they shall make gardens and eat their fruit. I will plant them on their land, and they shall never again be uprooted out of the land that I have given them," says the LORD your God. (Amos 9.13-15 ESV)*

In the days of the messianic kingdom, the curse of the fall ("by the sweat of your face you shall eat bread" - Genesis 3.19) will be broken, and the land will be fruitful, so fruitful that the one who reaps will overtake the one who plants. And the messianic kingdom will have no end.

> *And I will make for them a covenant on that day with the beasts of the field, the birds of the heavens, and the creeping things of the ground. And I will abolish the bow, the sword, and war from the land, and I will make you lie down in safety. And I will betroth you to me forever. I will betroth you to me in righteousness and in justice, in steadfast love and in mercy. I will betroth you to me in faithfulness. And you shall know the LORD. And in that day I will answer, declares the LORD, I will answer the heavens, and they shall answer the earth, and the earth shall answer the grain, the wine, and the oil, and they shall answer Jezreel, and I will sow her for myself in the land. And I will have mercy on No Mercy, and I will say to Not My People, 'You are my people'; and he shall say, 'You are my God.' (Hosea 2.18-23 ESV)*

In the day of the Lord, nation will no longer rise up against nation. Instruments of war will be abolished for they will not be needed. Everyone everywhere will lie down in safety. The messiah will rule in righteousness, justice, steadfast love, and mercy. And all of nature will enter into an eternal, faithful covenant with God.

The Minor Prophets indeed whet our appetite for the coming kingdom of God. And we can only see the glory of the eternal kingdom as we keep in mind the depravity of this world. The injustice of Israel so decried by the prophets makes us long for the kingdom ruled in righteousness, the home where righteousness dwells.

We would do well to read the Minor Prophets and allow them to create hunger pains for the coming kingdom of God.

Dr. Todd Pylant

# MICAH SPEAKS TODAY

About a day's walk from the city of Jerusalem lay the small village of Moresheth. And somewhere in that sleepy little town, baby boy Micah was brought into the world. It was a strange and turbulent time to live in the nation of Judah. Judah was a small fish in a big pond, and there were powerful sharks in that pond that seemed to always be on the hunt. To the southwest was Egypt. To the northeast was Assyria. And caught in the middle were the twin sisters of Israel and Judah.

We don't know what Micah did for a living, whether he was a shepherd or a craftsman. And we know nothing about his family. And we know nothing about how the Lord called him to be a prophet. In fact, Micah is never actually identified as a prophet. But what we do know is that he was filled with power and with the Spirit of the Lord and sent by God to deliver a message.

He lived a long life, and served the Lord as a messenger for a long time. He started preaching during the days of King Jotham and kept on preaching through the reign of Hezekiah, perhaps as long as 25 years.

Jotham was a righteous king, and he ordered his ways before the Lord his God. As a result, his reign was blessed. But during his reign, the people continued to follow the corrupt practices and the worship of pagan gods.

His son, Ahaz, was the opposite. Ahaz did not do what was right in the eyes of the Lord and multiplied the worship of pagan gods in Judah. He even practiced child sacrifice by offering his own sons as an offering to Baal. The land was corrupted under his leadership for 16 long years.

But Jotham's grandson was different. Even though Ahaz was evil, his son Hezekiah did what was right in the eyes of the Lord. Hezekiah cleansed the temple from all the idol worship that Ahaz had corrupted it with, and he restored the proper worship of the Lord and the celebration of the Passover. Hezekiah led the nation in a spiritual revival.

Micah was called by the Lord to speak His words during these back and forth days of Judah. At the beginning of his ministry, the nation had a righteous king but the people still worshipped other gods. In the middle of his ministry, the nation had an evil king who led the people into unspeakable depravity. At the end of his ministry, the nation had a righteous king who tried to lead the people back to the pure worship of the Lord. What would God have the man of God say to a nation like that?

To make matters worse, towards the end of his ministry, Judah experienced a national tragedy so great that it threatened their very existence. The powerful nation of Assyria had invaded the northern kingdom of Israel. Israel had fallen completely and hopelessly to the cruel Assyrians. But the Assyrians were not satisfied with that conquest. They continued to march on the southern kingdom of Judah. Their armies swallowed up village after village, most likely even Micah's hometown. And then they arrived at the gates of Jerusalem to destroy the capital city as well.

And in this moment of national despair, Hezekiah, the King of Judah, remembered the words of Micah the prophet. And the words of Micah led the king to repent of his sin and to seek the Lord to deliver Jerusalem. And the Lord answered his prayer.

Micah labored for 25 years, calling the people of Judah to repent of their sins so that they would be spared the judgment of God. But he also spoke words of hope and restoration, painting a picture of the blessings of the Lord should they return to Him.

Micah's ministry did not stop with his impact on King Hezekiah. Micah continues to impact the people of God today. God continues to speak through the prophet to His people today if we are willing to listen.

I have tried over the course of this book to help you understand the historical setting of the Minor Prophets. I hope I have helped you to understand their message in general but also the individual message of each Minor Prohet. And I have tried to give you some helpful hints about how to read the Minor Prophets to make them profitable to you today.

Finally, I want to take all that information and apply it to one particular Minor Prophet, our good friend Micah from the village of Moresheth. My goal is certainly NOT to write a comprehensive commentary on the book of Micah. That would be beyond the scope of this project, not to mention way beyond the scope of my abilities. Besides, there are several good commentaries on Micah, some of which are listed under "Resources" at the end of this book.

My goal is to demonstrate how the Minor Prophets can still be profitable for teaching, correction, training, and equipping the followers of Christ today. In the pages that follow, I will be exploring the following questions:

> *Micah was the rare successful prophet in that the people actually repented in response to his ministry. What can we learn about seeking spiritual awakening in our own land? And what do we learn about making spiritual renewals a long term change?*
>
> *Micah clearly called the people of God to do justice and love kindness. What can we learn specifically about doing justice through Micah? How can we apply that to today?*
>
> *Micah echoed the psalmist who wrote that the anger of the Lord is but for a moment but His favor lasts a lifetime (see Psalm 30.5). What can we learn about Micah's hopeful words about restoration? How does Micah point us toward the joy that comes in the morning?*
>
> *Micah had some strong words of condemnation for the failures of all of the pillars of society, both governmental powers and spiritual leaders. What can we learn about the role of religious leaders, organized religion, government, and the justice system from Micah?*
>
> *Micah painted a very clear picture of the eternal kingdom of God yet to come. We minimize heaven when we call it "a better place" when in reality the biblical portrait is that heaven is a divine place. What can we learn about heaven from the prophet Micah?*
>
> *Micah's name itself asks the question, "Who is like our God?" And the book ends with that same question (see Micah 7.18). What can we learn about the character of God through the entire prophetic ministry of the prophet Micah?*

I hope you will join me as we explore these great themes from Micah and see how it continues to be the inspired Word of God.

# LONGING FOR SPIRITUAL AWAKENING

In his most famous novel, author Miguel Cervantes chronicled the adventures of Alonso. Alonso was guilty of reading way too many chivalric romances, so many that he lost his sanity and tried to live out the characters in the stories he read. At one point, he declared himself a knight on the mission of restoring chivalry, and he took on the name of Don Quixote. After recruiting a sidekick, Don set out to live a knightly story. At one point, he discovered some thirty or forty giants with long arms. Unfortunately, his romantic delusions had corrupted his vision. He was only chasing windmills.

Thanks to Don, we now refer to people who attack imaginary enemies as "tilting at windmills." Sometimes, we even use the phrase to refer to those in a vain effort against adversaries real or imagined. The giants are simply too large. The battle is useless. Any effort is just "tilting at windmills."

Was Micah just tilting at windmills?

The Minor Prophets as a group spent almost 400 years calling the people of God to repentance and failed. They even laced their calls to repentance with visions of the impending judgment, and they still failed. And since they also spoke of the promise of restoration after the judgment, it's as if they knew they were going to fail. They knew they were tilting at windmills.

The prophet Jonah was a rare exception. The city of Nineveh repented when they heard his unwilling, eight word sermon. The repentance didn't last for long, but Jonah did get to reap the positive response to his message.

The prophet Micah proclaimed the word of the Lord for about 25 years. His ministry began during the reign of King Jotham (750 to 735 BC) and finished during the reign of King Hezekiah (715 to 687 BC). And Micah was one of those rare prophets who was finally able to taste success during the days of Hezekiah.

When the king of Assyria invaded the northern kingdom of Israel, his army continued to march south and threatened to defeat the southern kingdom of Judah as well. The army of Assyria made it all the way down to Jerusalem and lay siege to the city. They had the city shut up like a bird in a cage.

The Bible tells this story in 2 Kings 18-19, and in that story the prophet Isaiah encouraged King Hezekiah to trust in the Lord, to seek His face, and to trust that God would deliver the city. Hezekiah did so, and the Lord sent an angel of destruction into the Assyrian army that night. The next morning, the soldiers who had survived the night packed up and returned to Assyria. Jerusalem was saved.

Though the prophet Micah is not mentioned by the writer of 2 Kings, his part in this story was mentioned in the book of Jeremiah. Years later, when the beleaguered prophet Jeremiah was arrested and threatened with death, some of the religious leaders remembered the story of Hezekiah and used it in the defense of Jeremiah:

> Then the officials and all the people said to the priests and the prophets, "This man does not deserve the sentence of death, for he has spoken to us in the name of the LORD our God." And certain of the elders of the land arose and spoke to all the assembled people, saying, "Micah of Moresheth prophesied in the days of Hezekiah king of Judah, and said to all the people of Judah: 'Thus says the LORD of hosts, '"Zion shall be plowed as a field; Jerusalem shall become a heap of ruins, and the mountain of the house a wooded height.' Did Hezekiah king of Judah and all Judah put him to death? Did he not fear the LORD and entreat the favor of the LORD, and did not the LORD relent of the disaster that he had pronounced against them? But we are about to bring great disaster upon ourselves." (Jeremiah 26.16-19 ESV)

Notice that the city leaders quoted the words of warning of the prophet Micah (see Micah 3.12) as being credited with bringing Hezekiah to repentance and leading him to trust in the Lord. Isaiah and Micah were contemporary prophets, and some of their words were very similar. And in this story, Isaiah was the one who interpreted or applied or explained Micah's words to the king, but Micah was the prophet who preached repentance and was successful.

In this respect, Micah is profitable to us today for two reasons.

**First, Calling For Spiritual Awakening Takes Time.**

After two decades of calling the people of God to return to the Lord, his prophetic words finally found their target: the heart of the king of Judah. Hezekiah feared the Lord, sought God's favor, and the Lord delivered Jerusalem.

Most spiritual awakenings in world history have been preceded by a small group of people praying for a long period of time. I could give you example after example, but I will share the short story of the Hebrides Revival.

The islands of the Hebrides lie off the coast of Scotland. Two elderly sisters, both blind and disabled, could not attend church. But they could pray. And in 1949, they began to pray for a spiritual awakening in their land. After receiving a vision from the Lord, they urged the local pastor to send for a revival preacher, one Duncan Campbell. Not much happened at the first meeting, but the Spirit fell at the second meeting. When the service was over, the people didn't leave. They stayed all night praying and singing and crying out for revival.

As the news of the revival spread, people from neighboring towns began to arrive on buses. Work and daily chores were set aside as people gathered in homes, barns, and even by the roadside to pray and find the Lord. Confession and mass conversions were the order of the day. Campbell preached in churches and in open fields, often as many as eight times a day. The awakening continued into the early 1960s. And it all began because two elderly ladies committed themselves to pray for an extended period of time.

For those who are praying for children or grandchildren to come to saving faith, for those who are sharing the gospel with a close friend, and for those who are praying for a fresh move of God in their own land, Micah encourages us to keep praying, to keep sharing, to keep seeking. The fruit we seek may be long coming, but don't give up.

**Second, Moments Of Spiritual Victory Must Be Followed By Faithfully Walking With The Lord.**

But we are reminded that Micah's prophetic success story did not last forever. The spiritual awakening of Hezekiah and Jerusalem was soon followed by the abject pagan reign of his son, Manasseh. The revival of Hezekiah was followed by a rebellion against the Lord that included child sacrifice and setting up pagan altars in the Most Holy Place of the temple. Manasseh led the people of Judah to do more evil than all the pagan nations who had ever lived on that land. Combined.

Micah reminds us that our spiritual mountain top experiences must be followed with faithfulness in the day to day. We must walk with the Lord daily, obeying all of His commands and seeking His face. The emotional highs of religious victories fade quickly if there is no foundation of a sustaining relationship with Him. The mountain tops are often followed by the valleys, and we must keep walking faithfully through the valleys or else the victories will turn into defeats. Mountain top experiences are easy to endure. Walking with God in the day to day is hard to do.

And the success of Micah demonstrates that the true gospel must be passed down to each new generation. We must make disciples of those who come behind us. It is not enough to assume that they will walk faithfully with the Lord because of what they have seen. The primary mission of every generation is to make disciples who can make disciples because we are always one generation away from being a pagan land.

Dr. Todd Pylant

# GOD WANTS US TO LOVE JUSTICE

The one verse from the book of Micah that is most well-known is Micah 6.8:

> *He has told you, O man, what is good; and what does the LORD require of you but to do justice, and to love kindness, and to walk humbly with your God? (Micah 6.8 ESV)*

As we have already seen, the Minor Prophets consistently called the people of God to love justice, to do justice, and to work for justice. This was not just the work of Micah, but Micah does call the people of God to embrace God's heart for justice, and he described injustice very clearly. Injustice is:

> *Devising wickedness (Micah 2.1)*

> *Coveting the field and house of another and scheming to take it (Micah 2.2)*

> *Stealing another's inheritance (Micah 2.2)*

> *Mistreating widows (Micah 2.9)*

> *Hating the good and loving the evil (Micah 3.2)*

> *Taking bribes (Micah 3.11) as judges and other government officials (Micah 7.3)*

> *Using deceitful business practices like deceitful scales (Micah 6.11)*

> *Speaking lies (Micah 6.12)*

There are many voices crying out for justice today, and rightfully so. But we often think of justice as "the other guy's problem." But Micah puts God's love for justice squarely in the middle of everyday life. How we do business is a matter of justice.

How we personally treat widows and orphans and others in distress is a matter of justice. Simply hating the evil and loving the good is a matter of justice. Speaking the truth in love in all that we say is a matter of justice. And fighting the sinful desire of greed in our own hearts is a matter of justice.

Why is loving kindness and doing justice so important to the Lord? To answer that question, we only need to think about how the most powerful One in all the universe used His power. As the Creator and Sustainer of all things looked upon His creation, a creation filled with humans who constantly rebel against His commands and will, what did the Lord do? The words of the apostle Paul to the church in Philippi capture this so well:

> *Have this mind among yourselves, which is yours in Christ Jesus, who, though he was in the form of God, did not count equality with God a thing to be grasped, but emptied himself, by taking the form of a servant, being born in the likeness of men. And being found in human form, he humbled himself by becoming obedient to the point of death, even death on a cross. (Philippians 2.5-8 ESV)*

God the Son used His authority and power to serve sinful humanity by bearing their sins on the cross. And the Bible calls us to have this same mind, the mind of Christ. And when we take our power and authority and use it to mistreat others, we are offending the very nature of God.

Micah makes it very clear how important justice is to our God. What does God want from us? Burnt offerings? Our firstborn son? No. God wants us to do justice and to love kindness. Notice that God wants us to act and to love. To do justice concerns the actions that we take in a given moment, but to love kindness concerns our heart. God wants people who love justice and kindness just as much as He does. And until we get there, we will continue to fall short of the glory of God.

# JOY COMES IN THE MORNING

The reason I called this book *Grumpy Old Men* is because that is my general impression of the Minor Prophets. As a group, they seem to stand in the middle of the Old Testament and scream, "Get off my lawn." Without a closer reading, it seems as if the Minor Prophets offer little more than expressions of how much God hates sinners.

But Micah leaves us with a much clearer image of God's holiness and mercy. The book ends with this incredible message:

> *Who is a God like you, pardoning iniquity and passing over transgression for the remnant of his inheritance? He does not retain his anger forever, because he delights in steadfast love. He will again have compassion on us; he will tread our iniquities underfoot. You will cast all our sins into the depths of the sea. You will show faithfulness to Jacob and steadfast love to Abraham, as you have sworn to our fathers from the days of old.*
> *(Micah 7.18-20 ESV)*

After all the words of condemnation and judgment, Micah reminds us that the Lord does not retain His anger forever. In fact, the Lord delights in steadfast love. His anger is but for a moment, but His favor is for a lifetime (see Psalm 30.4-5). Despite all of our great sins, He will have compassion and cast our sins into the depths of the sea.

Forgiveness and restoration will come.

Micah not only ends the book with these words of hope, but they are laced throughout the book intentionally and skillfully. The book is divided into three major sections. Each section is introduced with the verb "to hear" (Micah 1.3, Micah 3.1, Micah 6.1). And each section has a warning of judgment followed by the promise of restoration.

Section one (chapters 1-2) begins by describing the horrors of the coming judgment as the Lord comes down from His holy temple in judgment (Micah 1.2). But it ends with the promise that the Lord will gather the remnant of Israel like sheep in a fold (Micah 2.12).

Section two (chapters 3-5) begins with the warning that Jerusalem shall become a heap of ruins (Micah 3.12) but ends with the glorious promise of the peace of the messianic kingdom. In that day, the messiah will rule the nations from Jerusalem and nations shall no longer go to war with other nations (Micah 4.3).

Section three (chapter 6-7) begins with the warning that God will strike Judah with a grievous blow (Micah 6.13) but ends with the promise that the Lord will once again show steadfast love to the children of Abraham (Micah 7.20).

The message of Micah, indeed the structure of the book itself, declares the mercy of God, the desire of God to forgive and redeem. Yes, the Lord was angry with their sinfulness, but His greater desire is to redeem and restore.

Weeping may tarry for the night, but joy comes in the morning!

# PILLARS OF SOCIETY

The condemnation of the prophet is most prolific upon the pillars of society, specifically the leaders of government and the religious leaders.

As we have already said, Micah calls the people of God to love and do justice. But he also speaks very strong words about those who are entrusted with the positions of enacting justice in society through the government and the court system. Micah condemns the judges and other governmental officials who conspire to take fields and houses and even inheritances away from the poor and powerless (Micah 2.2). This could only be done through a corrupted legal system. In Micah's day, the instruments of justice handed out rulings for bribes (Micah 3.11). God expected the rulers of the house of Israel to know justice, to love the good and hate the evil (Micah 3.1-2). Instead, they used their power to tear off the skin of the people of Israel.

Micah makes it clear that the abuse of power is no small sin in the eyes of the Lord. Whenever we are given the authority to enact justice, whether it be in government or in the workplace or even in the home, those who abuse power and fail to love justice fall under the judgment of God. And above all, the people of God who have experienced the loving justice of God in their own lives should be leading the charge to share that mercy and justice with others. Judah failed in this, and that failure continues in our own society today.

Micah also had very strong words to speak against the religious leaders of Judah, both priests and prophets. God put the religious leaders in place to teach the people the laws of God and of the covenant, and He appointed prophets to speak the word of the Lord to the people. But both failed miserably in Judah.

For starters, the priests and prophets bore some responsibility for the mass worship of pagan gods. The people had multiplied pagan altars partly because of the failure of the priests and prophets to uphold the truth. The prophets did not speak the word of the Lord but only spoke what they were paid to say (Micah 3.5). They were preachers for hire, not caring about the truthfulness of their sermons. Both the priests and the prophets taught for a price (Micah 3.11). They said what the people wanted to hear, and they failed to call the people to covenantal faithfulness.

Micah's condemnations are certainly profitable for us today. In a culture where prosperity preachers preach that God is a tool we can use to get what we really want, which is worldly riches, Micah calls us back to biblical and covenantal faithfulness. God is not some power we manipulate for money. Jesus was right, we cannot love both God and money.

Whereas the apostles taught believers to take up our cross and follow Jesus, to suffer for the sake of the kingdom, to consider the suffering of this world to be of no compare to the riches yet to come, the false prophets and religious leaders focus our delight in the treasures of this world. And to them, a god who would call them to sacrifice and trials and suffering is not delightful at all. Those who preach God as a tool for the American dream sell the most books. The same was true in the days of Micah, and the same is true today.

Micah demonstrates what happens to a society when the pillars of society fail. When those in authority abuse their authority and pervert justice, and when the religious leaders tickle ears and forsake the truth of God, the foundations of society implode. The judgment of God is to allow us to reap what we sow, to sow to the wind and reap the whirlwind (see Hosea 8.7). But make no mistake, the hand of the Lord will also rise up against the nations who pervert justice and truth.

# THE HOPE OF THE MESSIANIC KINGDOM

All of the Minor Prophets help us to understand and experience the hope of the coming messianic kingdom, and Micah is no different. In fact, Micah is perhaps most helpful in teaching us about the messianic kingdom and stirring hope within our hearts.

One of the many challenges of reading the prophetic books is discerning about which time period the prophet was speaking. Was the prophet speaking of the restoration after the exile? Was the prophet speaking about the first coming of the messiah? Was the prophet speaking about the new covenant age? Or was the prophet speaking of the second coming of the messiah and the messianic kingdom? The answer to those questions is sometimes more difficult to discover than others (as in the middle chapters of Isaiah), and Micah is no different.

For instance, in chapter four, Micah speaks of the mountain of the Lord. And on this mountain, the house of God will be raised up above all other nations. The nations will come to Jerusalem and ask to learn the ways of the Lord. And on that mountain, the messiah will judge between many nations as peace breaks out on all the earth. Weapons will be turned into agricultural instruments because they will no longer be needed in a time of universal peace. War will be a thing of the past. Everyone will dwell in peace. But the section curiously ends with the observation that the people of God will walk in the name of the Lord even as other peoples walk in the name of other gods.

So, of what time period is the prophet speaking?

Some have suggested that the prophet was looking forward to the age of missions where the gospel would go forth into all the world, but the missionary age has certainly not brought about the end of war. Others have suggested that the prophet was describing the messianic kingdom where other nations exist who need to learn about the Lord. Still others suggest that Micah was talking about the eternal heaven as described in Revelation 21.

This is a perfect example of the richness of the prophetic material, for all the answers are right to some degree. The prophet may have been speaking about the new covenant age, the messianic kingdom, and the eternal heaven at the same time. What is clear is that our longing for peace, our longing for the messiah to rule the nations, our longing for true justice, and our longing for all people to seek to live under the commands of God is something that will be fulfilled in the return of the messiah. Micah fuels our messianic hope and expectancy.

There are many and good scholars who would advocate that this section of Micah speaks to the eternal kingdom of God, what we think of as heaven. And I am not going to attempt to rebuff each of their very good explanations. But I would like to invite you to consider the words of Micah 4 as a word about the earthly reign of Christ.

In the vision given to John and recorded in the book of Revelation, John saw thrones and the resurrected martyrs reigning with Christ for a 1000 years:

> *Then I saw thrones, and seated on them were those to whom the authority to judge was committed. Also I saw the souls of those who had been beheaded for the testimony of Jesus and for the word of God, and those who had not worshiped the beast or its image and had not received its mark on their foreheads or their hands. They came to life and reigned with Christ for a thousand years. The rest of the dead did not come to life until the thousand years were ended. This is the first resurrection. Blessed and holy is the one who shares in the first resurrection! Over such the second death has no power, but they will be priests of God and of Christ, and they will reign with him for a thousand years. (Revelation 20:4-6 ESV)*

We refer to this as the "millennial reign of Christ," or the messianic kingdom on earth. This is distinct from the eternal kingdom of God as described in Revelation 21, i.e., the new heavens and the new earth. There is much debate about this thousand year reign of Christ, whether it is symbolic or not. And some are quick to point out that Revelation 20 is the only place in Scripture where a thousand year reign of Christ is described.

Or is it?

The Minor Prophets and other Old Testament prophets often describe the messianic kingdom in ways that can only fit the new heaven and the new earth. But there are also some times where the Minor Prophets describe the messianic kingdom in such a way that it can only be fulfilled in the earthly reign of the messiah.

And Micah 4 may be just one of those passages.

Consider the earthly reign of Christ in Revelation 20. Notice that this reign is before Satan is cast in the lake of fire for day and night forever (Revelation 20.7-10). And it is before the judgment of the Great White Throne (Revelation 20.11-15). And it is before the first heaven and first earth have passed away. And it is before all things are made new (Revelation 21.1-5). What might it look like for Christ to reign on earth for a period before all these things take place?

It might look like Micah 4.

When Christ reigns on earth, He will rule the nations from the mountain of the Lord, Jerusalem. It will be lifted up above all other mountains (Micah 4.1). He will judge between the nations, even strong nations far away (Micah 4.3). By His authority and power, He will bring peace on earth. Nations will no longer go to war (Micah 4.3). Under the reign of Christ, the curse of Genesis 3.17 (the curse on the land) will be broken. The land will be so fruitful that every person will sit under his own vine and fig tree (Micah 4.4). There will people on the earth who follow other gods (Micah 4.5), but people from all the nations on the earth will come to Jerusalem to be taught His ways and to walk in His paths (Micah 4.2).

The earthly reign of Christ, as described in Micah 4, will usher in an age of peace, an age where the world recognizes the Lord as the one true God, an age of justice and righteousness. But until Satan is banished forever, and before all things are made new, this peaceful reign of the messiah on earth will be short lived until the work of redemption is completed.

The words of Micah cause the people of God to long for the messianic kingdom. John said that those who were part of the earthly rule of Christ were "blessed." And now we can see why.

# GODLY PATRIOTISM

Micah also challenges us to think about what it means to be patriotic.

Patriotism is simply love for or devotion towards one's country. And the temptation was always for the prophets to only speak prophetic words of blessing upon the home team. Amos was chastised for preaching against Israel. The religious and political leaders told him outright to never again prophesy against the city of Bethel in Israel because it was the king's sanctuary, and it was a temple of the kingdom (see Amos 7.13).

In other words, some religious and political leaders think that patriotism requires that a prophet only speak favorable words about one's own nation. Micah himself chastised those false prophets who would only preach "Peace" because that is what they were paid to say (Micah 3.5). The false prophets, if paid the correct amount of money, would always give the encouraging message that "No disaster shall come upon us" (Micah 3.11 ESV). The people told him to not preach of such things as the wrath of God. "Disgrace will not overtake us!" (Micah 2.6 ESV).

But is preaching peace when disaster is coming really love and devotion for one's country? Or is it more loving and patriotic to stand in the gates and plead for the people to return to the Lord so that His judgment might be averted?

The prophet knew that the Lord had a righteous indictment against His people (Micah 6.2). Micah knew that the lord was coming out of His holy place because of the transgression of the house of Israel (Micah 1.3-5). But it did not please the prophet to declare such things. He did not walk about the city shouting of the judgment to come with glee in his voice. No, he went about stripped and naked, making "lamentation like the jackals and mourning like the ostriches" (Micah 1.8 ESV). It grieved his heart that the nation he loved had wandered so far away from the Lord. But he loved the Lord more than he loved his nation. And he loved the ways of the Lord more than he loved his country. And if his country chose to walk away from the Lord, the prophet would choose to walk with the Lord.

Micah reminds us that when the church loses its prophetic voice, a nation falls into a perilous condition. When the church loves the kingdom of this world more than the kingdom of God and can only preach "peace" and "no destruction will overcome you," then it loses its voice to call the nation to return to the Lord. We must be able to identify injustice. We must be willing to call out idolatry. We must be willing to point out immorality. But not with gleeful hearts as if we enjoy consigning people to hell. The steadfast love of the Lord will not allow that. The mercy of God will not allow that.

But the holiness of God will not allow His people to ignore the rebellion of God's people either, or the rebellion of a nation.

Godly patriotism is a love for country that is so deep that we realize that our only national hope is to walk faithfully with the Lord. And when the national conscience turns away from the Lord, a patriotic heart is grieved and mourns. The patriotic heart cries out for the nation he loves to return to the Lord. The patriot stands in the gates and warns of the judgment that might come should we keep running away from the Lord.

In the end, godly patriotism agrees with the words of the Lord to the prophet Micah, "Make yourself bald and cut off your hair for the children of your delight. Make yourself bald as the eagle for they shall go from you into exile" (Micah 1.16 ESV). God was telling the prophet to grieve deeply for the words he was commanded to say were both true and horrible at the same time. They shall go from you into exile.

# WHO IS LIKE OUR GOD?

The prophetic book of Micah begins and ends with one question. The book begins with the name of the prophet which means, "Who is Like God?" And the book ends with the question once again, "Who is a God like you?"

What one characteristic of God most distinguishes the Lord from all other gods?

> *Who is a God like you, pardoning iniquity and passing over transgression for the remnant of his inheritance? He does not retain his anger forever, because he delights in steadfast love. He will again have compassion on us; he will tread our iniquities underfoot. You will cast all our sins into the depths of the sea. (Micah 7.16-19 ESV)*

At the end of the day, the Lord is most unique for His mercy.

All other gods are believed to have some degree of power. And some gods are evil, and some gods are good. Some gods like Baal control the fruitfulness of crops and cattle. Other gods are believed to control the sky and the rain. The idea of a divine being with power is not unique to the Lord.

What is unique to the God of Israel is that He is merciful. He pardons iniquity. He delights in steadfast love. He will cast all our sins into the depths of the sea. No other pagan god was like that.

The Canaanites worshiped the Baal god so that their crops and cattle and women would be fertile. They offered sacrifices, sometimes animal and sometimes human, all in an effort to make the gods happy so the crops would grow, their herds would increase, and their family tree would enlarge.

While the idea of "sin" might not have been unique to the Lord, He certainly is unique in His mercy. Notice that Micah did not rejoice in the hope that we as humans could do something to make our sin go away. No. The wonder of the One True God is that He Himself will cast all our sins into the depths of the sea (see Micah 7.19).

Micah foreshadows the depths of the mercy of God as revealed in Jesus. Because God is rich in mercy, He did something for us that our sins might be cast into the depths of the sea forever. Through the cross, our sins were trampled underfoot by the steadfast love of the Lord. Through the blood of Jesus, God has pardoned our iniquity and passed over our transgression.

In the old covenant, sinners would bring a lamb to the temple as an offering for their sin. They would lay their hands on the lamb and confess their sins. Their sins would be transferred to the lamb, and the lamb would die in the sinner's place. The Lord was gracious and accepted it as atonement for their sin.

But God is even more merciful than accepting an innocent lamb to die in our place. God sent His Son, Jesus, to become the Lamb of God who takes away our sin. When Jesus stretched out His arms and allowed the soldiers to drive the nails into His hands, the Lord was pleased to accept His death as atonement for our sins.

When we put our faith in Jesus Christ as our Savior and Lord, we are essentially laying our hands on the head of the Lamb of God. We confess our sins, and our sins are transferred onto Him. And by grace through faith, His righteousness is transferred onto us.

Who is a God like YHWH? Who is a God who would ever think of becoming sin for sinners so that sinners could become righteous? Who is like our God who Himself bore our sins so that we might be forgiven? Who is like our God who became the once for all sacrifice, the once for all Lamb of God to take away our sin?

The God of Israel.

The Lord alone is a merciful God.

# FINAL WORDS

At the end of the day, I hand the Book of the Twelve to you in a protective plastic bag. You have come to me and asked for the Bible. You have come with a problem to be solved or a need to be met. You have searched the shelves of self-help books. You have gone through your favorite memory verses that have always made you feel good in the past.

But the problem just won't go away.

And now, in desperation, you are willing to take extreme measures. You are looking for that one solution that will really attack your problem. You are a little desperate but also a little hopeful. Perhaps someone knows something you don't know.

So, I hand you the Minor Prophets.

But I don't hand them to you glibly. I don't give them to you like it is just another broom or mop or cleaning product. No. This one is different. You really need to read the warning label.

I know you have ignored the Minor Prophets for most of your life, but it is time to read them now.

I know you have never given them the energy required to understand them, but you are desperate now.

I know you have no idea what truth, what wisdom, what guidance lies between the pages of the Minor Prophets, but they are calling to you today.

You really need to read the warning label.

You really need to read the Minor Prophets.

# RESOURCES

Boice, James Montgomery. *The Minor Prophets: An Expositional Commentary*. Grand Rapids: Baker Books, 1986.

Chalmers, Aaron. *Interpreting the Prophets: Reading, Understanding and Preaching from the Worlds of the Prophets*. Downers Grove: InterVarsity Press, 2013.

*ESV Study Bible*, Crossway Publishing, 2008.

Fuhr, Richard Alan and Gary E. Yates. *The Message of the Twelve: Hearing the Voice of the Minor Prophets*. Nashville: B&H Academic Publishers, 2016.

Pylant, Todd. *Understanding the Bible and Making It Profitable*. Benbrook: Word of God Speak Publishing, 2015.

# OTHER BOOKS BY TODD PYLANT

*Understanding the Bible and Making It Profitable (2015)*

*The Diary of a Future Sufferer (2015)*

*D14: A Strategy for Making Disciples Who Make Disciples (2013)*

*If: The Conditionality of the Gospel and the Danger of Apostasy (2012)*

*Word of God Speak: Understanding the Bible and Making It Profitable (2011)*

Printed in Great Britain
by Amazon